PHILIP THE FAIR AND BONIFACE VIII

Second Edition

PHILIP THE FAIR
AND BONIFACE VIII

State vs. Papacy

Edited by **CHARLES T. WOOD**
Dartmouth College

HOLT, RINEHART AND WINSTON
New York • Chicago • San Francisco • Atlanta
Dallas • Montreal • Toronto • London • Sydney

Cover illustration: Detail of the tomb of Boniface VIII
in the Vatican grottoes by Arnolfo di Cambio. *(The
Granger Collection)*

CONTENTS

CHRONOLOGY

1073–1085	Pontificate of Gregory VII; foundations of papal monarchy laid.
January 1077	Humiliation of Henry IV by Gregory VII at Canossa.
1198–1216	Pontificate of Innocent III; high point of papal monarchy.
October 5, 1285	Philip the Fair becomes king of France.
April 4, 1292	Death of Nicholas IV, followed by papal interregnum of twenty-seven months.
July 5, 1294	Pietro di Murrone elected pope (Celestine V).
December 13, 1294	Celestine V renounces the papacy.
December 24, 1294	Benedict Gaetani elected pope (Boniface VIII).
February 24, 1296	In the bull *Clericis laicos* Boniface VIII forbids lay taxation of the clergy.
May 1296	Death of Celestine V.
August 1, 1296	Boniface declares the Spiritual Franciscans heretical.
August 17, 1296	Philip the Fair forbids exportation of gold and silver from France, thereby cutting papal revenues.
November 1296	French publicists begin attacking the pope.
February 7, 1297	In the bull *Romana mater* Boniface largely suspends *Clericis laicos* for France.
May 1297	The Colonnas begin revolt against Boniface.
June–August 1297	Boniface capitulates completely to Philip; the canonization of Louis IX, Philip's grandfather, is announced.
November 27, 1297	Boniface proclaims a crusade against the Colonnas.
March–June 1298	Boniface arbitrates Philip's Flemish war, but is allowed to do so only as Benedict Gaetani, a private person; his decision favors the French.
October 1298	Palestrina, home and last stronghold of the Colonnas, falls to papal troops; the Colonnas make their submission and are imprisoned.
June 1299	Boniface orders Palestrina razed, with its site put to the plow and sown with salt; the Colonnas escape and flee to France.
February 22, 1300	Boniface proclaims the Jubilee of 1300.

July 12, 1301	Bernard Saisset, bishop of Pamiers, is arrested for treason by Philip's agents.
October 1301	The trial of Saisset begins at Senlis.
December 4–5, 1301	Boniface orders Saisset set free and summons all French bishops to Rome for a council (to be held in November 1302) at which the king's government and the state of religion in France will be discussed; in *Salvator mundi* and *Ausculta fili* Boniface suspends all privileges of clerical taxation granted the French king and reproves Philip for his conduct.
April 10, 1302	Philip holds an assembly of clergy, nobles, and towns in Paris; all eventually support king versus pope.
July 11, 1302	The French army is disastrously beaten by the Flemings at Courtrai.
November 1302	The papal council opens at Rome with half the French bishops attending; *Unam Sanctam,* a strong statement of papal powers, is issued November 18.
February–March 1303	Philip holds new assemblies in Paris; a cautious attitude toward the pope is displayed.
March 7, 1303	Commission given Nogaret for secret mission to Italy.
March 12, 1303	Nogaret proclaims Boniface a usurper and heretic, and calls on Philip to help assemble a council to condemn Boniface and to elect a new pope; Philip consents.
June 13, 1303	Philip holds a third group of assemblies, at the Louvre, and strong attacks are made against Boniface; commissioners are subsequently dispatched to stir up the rest of France against the pope.
Mid-August 1303	It becomes known that Boniface plans to excommunicate Philip on September 8 at Anagni.
September 7, 1303	Nogaret and Sciarra Colonna storm Anagni and capture the pope, but are forced to flee two days later.
October 11, 1303	Death of Boniface VIII.
April 27, 1311	Clement V in *Rex Gloriae* praises Philip's zeal and good intentions in the struggle with Boniface; he orders quashed all of Boniface's bulls issued after November 1, 1300, that were offensive to the king.
November 29, 1314	Death of Philip the Fair.

Philip the Fair with his family. Manuscript illumination, fourteenth century.
(Bibliothèque Nationale, Cliché...)

INTRODUCTION

The Middle Ages have frequently been called the Age of Faith, but no one can study them for long without becoming aware of the tremendous tensions hidden beneath the surface. For, religious as medieval Europe undoubtedly was, its inhabitants often disagreed on the nature of their ·faith and on the way life should be organized and regulated so as best to achieve the kingdom of heaven. As a result, frequent conflict was the order of the day, and from time to time disputes became so intense in their ferocity that they threatened to destroy the Christian ordering of society. No dispute has attracted more widespread attention than the controversies that marred Church-State relations throughout the latter half of the Middle Ages.

To the modern mind these quarrels often appear to have been little more than attempts by one side to gain independence and mastery of the other, but the issues involved were in fact more complicated. The Europe that emerged after the dissolution of the Roman Empire in the West soon developed a social, intellectual, and political structure in which such clear-cut ambitions were impossible. Indeed, even to talk of the controversies as a problem in Church-State relations is somewhat misleading, as the Church and the State were so organized that it was impossible to say where one left off and the other began.

Much of this difficulty arose because of the emperor Constantine's acceptance of Christianity (313), for his action led to a situation in which a creative partnership between the Church and the secular government became a natural goal. Such cooperation did in fact occur, and although it was occasionally marred by sharp clashes and controversies, a basic alliance had been formed. Moreover, in the West the tendency toward amalgamation received added impetus because the laity, increasingly barbarized and illiterate, was forced to rely on the superior education of the clergy in order to carry out even the most elementary tasks of day-to-day administration. After the mid-ninth century the gradual feudalization of government slowly completed the process of integration by subjecting prelates and their lands to most of the feudal and vassalic obligations that characterized the organization of medieval Europe. These developments, already discernible under Charlemagne (768–814),

1

reached fullest flower in the German Empire where after the middle of the tenth century imperially selected bishops and abbots were charged with the administration of vast territories, thereby making them the central pivot of imperial rule.

Furthermore, the very nature of political thought encouraged the intertwining of Church and State. Kings and emperors enjoyed no purely secular authority; on the contrary, they like the pope ruled by the grace of God and in His stead. Because all power was of God, temporal rulers had a spiritual mission difficult to separate from that of the clergy. Theoretically, distinctions did exist, particularly in the writings of Pope Gelasius I (492–496), whose views formed the foundation for most later medieval thinking on the subject. For Gelasius, the spiritual Church and the temporal State were normally independent in their actions, but at the same time he was at pains to emphasize that the Church's authority *(auctoritas)* was superior to the State's power *(potestas)* and that the latter's ability to act really depended on a delegation of sovereignty from the former, which, given its otherworldly concerns, was understandably reluctant to soil its hands with earthly cares.

Gelasius notwithstanding, it proved difficult in practice to distinguish clearly between the role of the Church and that of the State. Gelasian dualism —what St. Bernard later called the two-swords theory—was fine as an idea, but it tended to crumble when confronted with the complexities of normal political life. If, for example, a ruler sensed that the Church or the papacy was falling into a state of moral decay, was it not his Christian duty, derived from his holy office, to intervene? Similarly, was not the pope bound to interfere, possibly with more justice, when he saw monarchs taking actions that might endanger their subjects' immortal souls?

It was from such problems, both practical and theoretical, that the controversies between the spiritual and temporal powers arose. Given the feudalization of society and the God-centeredness of thought, it is hardly surprising that the issues could never be successfully resolved in a manner satisfactory to both sides. Thus, when the emperor Henry III invaded Italy in the 1040s to rescue the papacy from the hands of three warring popes, the Church may have profited from his action, but it could never rid itself of the fear that temporal control by the emperor might prove a greater detriment to its spiritual aspirations and obligations than had the previously existing situation.

The reform program of Gregory VII (1073–1085) threatened to push the pendulum completely in the other direction. Wishing to purify the Church and to emancipate it from all taint of domination by the laity, Gregory embarked on a course designed to create an independent and wholly clerical Church led by a pope with virtually monarchical powers. When he encountered opposition, particularly from the emperor Henry IV (1056–1106), he stressed the view inherent in the Gelasian two-swords theory that the Church because it was concerned with ultimate things was superior to the State when they met in conflict: Henry's continued resistance was countered by a formal papal declaration of his deposition from office. Although Gregory's ambitions were never fully realized in his lifetime, he saw the balance clearly begin to swing toward the papacy, where it remained for two centuries.

In the thirteenth century the situation changed. As A. C. Flick describes it, the Church was then at the height of its power, its position buttressed by able popes, brilliant theologians, and a competent and wide-ranging administration. At the same time the face of Europe was being transformed: cities were rising, the economy was expanding, and the monarchies, particularly in France and England, were rapidly becoming national states. It is in this context, Flick states, that the last and greatest of the medieval Church-State disputes, that between Boniface VIII and Philip the Fair, must be viewed, for in taking on France Boniface was engaging in a battle with a power whose political conceptions and national self-awareness were increasingly modern in tone and wholly antithetical to the Church's hierarchical view of society. Hence—to use an example not employed by Flick—when Boniface proclaimed, "We hold both the swords," he found himself confronted with the response of Pierre Flote, Philip's minister, "True, Holy Father, but where your swords are but a theory, ours are a reality." Not surprisingly, then, this clash was the Church's undoing. In Flick's words, "[Boniface's] pontificate marks the beginning of the decline of the power and glory of the Medieval Papacy."

When the issues are more closely examined, however, they appear rather less simple than Flick's "modern State versus medieval Church" thesis would lead one to believe. As Adrien Baillet makes clear, the elevation of Benedict Gaetani to the pontificate as Boniface VIII in 1294 was anything but a normal event. The resignation of his predecessor, the saintly Celestine V, presented the Church with difficult problems, as such an event had never before occurred. Furthermore, since Boniface himself was intimately involved in Celestine's renunciation, doubts about his motives were quick to arise after his own elevation to the throne of St. Peter. Baillet, hostile to Boniface and all his works, makes the most of the situation to question subtly the new pope's legitimacy and the spirituality of his ambitions. No evidence has ever been discovered to support these charges, but they should not on that account be totally dismissed, for their very existence is illustrative of the tremendous pressures under which Boniface was forced to operate.

This is a theme much stressed by Philip Hughes, who presents a more sympathetic view of Boniface's accession. Unlike Baillet, he never doubts the new pope's legitimacy; rather, he accepts it and argues from fuller evidence that the Church needed precisely a pope of Boniface's talents to bring order out of the chaos that Celestine's otherworldly disregard of day-to-day administration had caused. These contrary interpretations are not entirely antithetical, but the reader must choose which to emphasize, for much of his understanding of later developments will depend upon his view here. If, for example, he doubts the genuineness of Boniface's spiritual motives, he will later be forced to decide whether Philip's attacks were aimed at the whole hierarchical conception of the Church, as Flick maintains, or simply at the pope himself, a man whose views were judged untenable under any conditions.

Early in his pontificate Boniface faced crises on several fronts. When in his bull *Clericis laicos* (1296) he forbade secular taxation of the clergy, both Edward I of England and Philip the Fair of France stoutly resisted, while in Italy the Colonna family, led by its two members—James and Peter—in the College of Cardinals, rose in almost simultaneous rebellion. Boniface was able momentarily to best the Colonnas, but he was forced to retreat before Edward's and Philip's onslaught, giving way on the matter of taxation and generally doing everything in his power to regain the French king's favor. Yet causation in these related attacks is far from clear. Edgar Boutaric's account would lead one to believe that Boniface surrendered to Philip only because he saw the Colonnas as the greater danger, whereas Charles-Victor Langlois argues that Philip had manipulated Italian affairs precisely to force Boniface into granting concessions. Here again the reader's choice of interpretations is important, since to opt for Boutaric's is greatly to diminish one's sense of the importance of French assertiveness and aggressiveness to the outcome; Philip's victory becomes little more than a by-product of a Roman quarrel fought within the Church.

Another aspect of the dispute is the possible illegitimacy of Boniface's election. The Colonnas had openly raised this issue in their feud with the pope, and if their position had been accepted, he might quickly have fallen from power, thus ending the quarrel. But it was not accepted, for, as Jean Leclercq convincingly demonstrates, the Colonnas' views were repeatedly rejected by the leading theologians of the University of Paris. Leclercq notes, however, that the arguments of the theologians frequently entertained the possibility of deposing a pope for manifest heresy. This was far from being a new theory, but the fact that it was raised at this time and in Paris may help to explain why the French attempted to use this approach when the struggle was renewed in 1301 and 1302.

Leclercq admits that even though the theologians of the University of Paris may have accepted Boniface's legitimacy, people at large may not have done so. Félix Rocquain agrees with this view and maintains that it may have been one of the lesser reasons behind Boniface's decision to hold the Papal Jubilee of 1300; moreover, it may help to explain why he displayed himself there with imperial splendor and made all-embracing claims to power. The Jubilee was the pinnacle of his career, and the outpourings of the faithful, not to mention the encouragement of Philip's enemies, confirmed him in his intransigence toward France. Hence, when Philip attempted to try one of his bishops for treason, Boniface's response was sharp and immediate. He again prohibited taxation of the clergy; he withdrew all the special temporal and spiritual privileges previously accorded the French; and in the bull *Ausculta fili* (1301) he underlined his duty and right to regulate the king's conduct.

The striking feature of Rocquain's interpretation is the extent to which it rests on the assumption that Boniface's actions were always the product of his strong personality reacting quite personally to the immediate situation. Philip Hughes takes a contrary view. Boniface was, after all, the pope, and Hughes is quick to emphasize the extent to which this office imposed on him the solemn obligation of defending the Church and its traditional rights and privileges. If Boniface chose to resist and deny the pretensions of the French, it was not because he was an obstinate old man whose pride had been kindled by the magnificence of the Jubilee and the blandishments of Philip's enemies. On the contrary, he was doing no more than his office demanded, and only after extreme provocation. No pope worthy of the name could possibly have done otherwise.

Be that as it may, *Ausculta fili* led to a harsh French reaction. Philip the Fair caused a forged and extreme version of this bull to be drawn up, circulated, and publicly burned. He then summoned assemblies of the clergy, nobles, and bourgeois of France in which he skillfully managed to obtain near-universal support for his opposition to what he viewed as papal infringements of his royal prerogatives. The culmination of the quarrel was fast approaching.

Boniface replied in the bull *Unam Sanctam* (1302), a document that many historians have described as being the most all-embracing statement of papal claims to universal temporal and spiritual authority ever issued. T. S. R. Boase tends to this view, supporting his case by reference both to the political context in which the bull was composed and to the writings of contemporary theorists whose thought *Unam Sanctam* frequently parallels. But Jean Rivière argues that most of the ideas in the document were in fact traditional and that to read extremism into its pronouncements is to overlook the caution with which they are stated.

Rivière may be right, but to accept his interpretation as the whole story would make incomprehensible the fierce steps taken by the French to counter this bull. First, William of Plaisians, a royal minister, brought charges of heresy against the pope; then, Philip dispatched William of Nogaret to Anagni where, with Colonna help, Boniface was seized and momentarily imprisoned. It would seem, then, that Boase's views must also be at least partially accepted, even by those inclining to the interpretation advanced by Rivière, for it is hard to believe that purely traditional ideas could have led to such an intemperate response.

Anagni is one of the great confrontations of history and has understandably attracted the greatest attention. One's estimate of it is necessarily conditioned by one's estimate of Boniface's character. If, like Adrien Baillet, one chooses to accept the worst about him, his treatment and death while an outrage to the papal office itself may nevertheless seem justified as an attack on the man. If one takes a more generous view and emphasizes some of the more constructive aspects of Boniface's pontificate, then, like T. S. R. Boase, one may be led to conclude that a tragedy occurred both for the man and for the papacy. Moreover, to accept Robert Fawtier's interpretation may be to extend this sense of tragedy to Nogaret himself, a man whom Fawtier views as having had no premeditated intention of assaulting the pope.

This incident—and all the crises leading up to it—cannot be fully understood until one grasps something of the character and aims of Philip the Fair. Here Charles-Victor Langlois presents the reader with an enigma, for he finds nothing in the extensive literary evidence of the period to suggest that Philip was anything more than a handsome, easy-going nonentity. This interpretation is vigorously challenged by Joseph R. Strayer who, resting his case on documentary evidence from the French Chancery, insists that Philip was a strong king whose true leadership has been obscured by his consistent tendency to delegate responsibility. One's decision will undoubtedly be based on one's reaction to the evidence advanced, but whichever view is accepted, it should be kept in mind that both imply the emergence of a bureaucratically organized, semimodern French state even as Flick initially maintained, for French policy could never have been pursued with such vigor and persistence without hosts of officials operating either at the king's command or in his place.

All this leads to the question of the ultimate significance of Boniface VIII and Philip the Fair in the long history of the Church and of its relations with the State. Since Boniface's pontificate was followed almost immediately by the so-called Babylonian Captivity (1305–1378), which for seventy years saw the popes residing at Avignon under watchful French surveillance, it is easy to understand why Flick should have regarded his reign as "the beginning of the decline of the power and glory of the Medieval Papacy." Indeed, since the Avignonese residency itself led directly to the Great Schism (1378–1415), in which Christendom was divided into warring camps headed by two, and sometimes three, hostile popes, Flick's indictment can be, and has been, extended. Never again was the Church to regain its universal prestige; rather, it was soon to find itself torn asunder, seemingly forever, by the hostile forces of the Protestant Reformation.

This is the point of view taken by Mandell Creighton in his *History of the Papacy from the Great Schism to the Sack of Rome.* For Creighton, the significance of Boniface's pontificate can be measured only against the broad tapestry of history, and when this is done, it becomes immediately apparent that his career marks a turning point: Boniface's defeat at Anagni is the great reversal of Gregory VII's humiliation of Henry IV in 1077 at Canossa, and it stands halfway in time between that first papal victory and those terrible days in 1527 when the largely Lutheran troops of the emperor Charles V subjected Rome to a two-week sack. In Creighton's mind the symbolism is suggestive, and while he quite properly refuese to place too much weight on this interpretation, it is nevertheless apparent that he regards the failings of Boniface VIII as a foreshadowing of the Reformation to come.

F. M. Powicke shows less willingness to paint so large a picture. In assessing Creighton's work fifty years after it was written, Powicke finds much to commend but at the same time uses his own considerable knowledge of medieval religious life and of the Church to modify the usual judgments of Boniface and of his role in the crises of his reign. Powicke readily admits Boniface's own personal weaknesses, but more than other historians of the period he emphasizes the extent to which the pope was operating within the context of a long historical tradition, one that shaped his actions and responses every bit as much as did his own impetuous personality. As a result, Boniface and his controversies with Philip the Fair take on a complexity of meaning that would seem to elude the easy generalizations of Creighton and Flick.

Furthermore, Powicke underlines his differences with earlier historians in another way when he states that his goal is to elucidate "the crowded scenes, the incessant variety of purpose, opinion and passion, amidst which Pope Boniface had to make himself felt." He sees no point in broad generalizations or in easy moralizing about the virtues and foibles of historical heroes and villains; such things are no more than "the ghostly refinements of reflection which we call the verdict of history." True history, he feels, involves an intensive study of the facts, for it is only through mastery of facts that one can begin to understand the motivations of men and hence why events happened as they did. In other words, Powicke maintains that the historian's duty and purpose are only to know the past, not to judge it. If this sage counsel is kept in mind, the reader should have few difficulties in coming to grips with the real issues surrounding the conflicts between Philip the Fair and Boniface VIII.

In the reprinted selections footnotes appearing in the original sources have in general been omitted unless they contribute to the argument or better understanding of the selection.

A. C. FLICK (1869–1942) was a historian of wide learning and interests whose published writing was almost equally divided between studies of the Middle Ages and of the politics of New York State. His two best-known books, *The Rise of the Mediaeval Church* and *The Decline of the Medieval Church*, together form a coherent statement of the traditional interpretation of the Church's place and role in medieval society. The following selection, which is taken from the latter work, not only places the quarrels of Boniface VIII and Philip the Fair within the broader context of thirteenth-century developments but also sheds light on one way of viewing the significance of Philip's assault on the papacy.*

A. C. Flick

The New Challenge
to Medieval Papalism

At the end of the thirteenth century the ecclesiastical empire of Rome was the widest in territorial extent that up to that time had been obtained under any of the Pontiffs. With the exception of southern Spain, the Pope's rule was unquestioned throughout all Central and Western Europe. At the same time plans were being made continually to recapture the places lost in the East.[1] Not only were overtures for unification made with the Armenians, the Russians, and the Greeks; but missionaries were also sent to labour among the Mongols, the Mohammedans, the Persians, and the Chinese. Meanwhile the obligation to wage a holy crusade against all infidels and heretics was ever kept vividly before the imaginations of the Christian princes.

Under the great Pope Innocent III (*d.* 1216) and his sixteen successors in the thirteenth century, upon the accession of Boniface VIII in the year 1294, the Medieval Church had attained the extreme limits of its power. Its dogma had been elaborated and accepted; its canon law had been developed and generally enforced; its hierarchical machinery for governmental purposes had been completed and was in full operation. The complete sway of the papal

---

[1] In 1291, Acre, the last Christian possession in the East, was lost.

*From A. C. Flick, *The Decline of the Medieval Church* (New York: Alfred A. Knopf, Inc., 1930), vol. 1, pp. 5–7, 8–9, 11–13, 15–17. Reprinted by permission of Routledge & Kegan Paul Ltd., London. Footnotes omitted.

monarchy over the Church had been universally recognized and the right of the Pope to interfere in the affairs of the European States had been established. With the overthrow of the Hohenstaufen emperors, the Pope stood forth in strong relief as the sole heir and representative of the claim of ancient Rome to universal rule.[2] This universality of papal supremacy was not only ably defended by keen ecclesiastical jurists, by the canon law, by the legislation of numerous councils, and by many historical precedents; but also by the brainiest theologians of the thirteenth century, such as Albertus Magnus, Duns Scotus, and Thomas Aquinas, who sought to prove that submission to the Roman Pontiff was required of every human being. Thomas Aquinas made the most sweeping statement of the papal theory when he asserted that, under the authority of the New Testament, kings must be subject to the Pope because he had the right to deprive heretical and schismatic rulers of all their authority and to release subjects from their civil obedience. The Angelic Doctor further asserted that Christ had invested the Pope with universal authority over the Church and hence he could not err; consequently it followed that the Church must rule the State, and hence the Church must be controlled by a monarchy sufficiently strong to preserve the unity of faith and to overthrow unbelievers. To enforce these pretensions a veritable papal army, both priestly and monkish, covered Christendom to carry out the Pope's will and to compel obedience to it. Thus the

Papacy with the finest organization since the days of Rome, defended by the keenest intellects of the Middle Ages, in possession of a powerful army obedient to every demand, with frightened princes ready to draw the sword for its defence against all enemies, internal or external, and with the credulous and intensely religious masses accepting its claims and prerogatives, was unquestionably the dominant power in European civilization in the thirteenth century.

The fact must be kept clearly in mind that during the thirteenth century the Roman Church consciously perpetuated the Imperial Roman Empire and sought to exercise its prerogatives to the point of monopoly. The theological literature of the day was full of illustrations of the Church as the lord, the soul, and the sun, while the State was the servant, the body, and the moon. As a result the century was replete with conflicts between the papal and secular powers, and, with the fall of the Hohenstaufen house, ended in the triumph of the papal hierarchy. Papal supremacy was well nigh undisputed. The kingdoms of Aragon, Portugal, Sicily, and England were papal fiefs; a Latin Empire had been established at Constantinople; the Armenians bowed to the authority of the Pope; France and Germany were submissive. The Pope, changed from the vicar of Peter to the vicar of Christ on earth, had become the real Roman Emperor, and held the law and peace of the world in his hand. . . .

On the surface of things, and to the short-sighted medieval ecclesiastical opportunist, it looked as if the papal system was everywhere triumphant. But certain forces were already appearing in Western Europe to dispute the lofty and sweeping claims of the Papacy and to weaken the tremendous power wielded

---

[2] The Hohenstaufens were the German rulers of the Holy Roman Empire. They warred frequently with the papacy, but their hopes of domination were ended by the death in 1250 of Frederick II, the last emperor from the line. —*Ed.*

by the head of the Roman Church. The causes which were undermining hierarchical authority and pretensions at this time were political, intellectual, economic, and social.

The power of the Medieval Church was due in a large measure to the absence of efficient secular rulers backed up by loyal subjects and an adequate military force. During the period of feudal anarchy the Church easily assumed the functions of the State in maintaining order, in administering justice, in caring for the unfortunate, and in encouraging industry and learning. Nor can anyone gainsay the invaluable service it rendered in these important fields. On the other hand, when the modern national states like France and England began to emerge and felt able to manage their own affairs, to protect their subjects in life and property, and to mete out justice, they attempted to make themselves politically independent of the clergy and the Pope. Educated laymen and civil lawyers became more numerous and gradually replaced the churchmen as counsellors and assistants to royalty. The rise of the national state and the new system of political science on which it rested, together with the able publicists who so successfully defended it, mark a most significant transition from the medieval era to the modern period in the history of Western Europe. This new force not only challenged the validity of the ground taken by Gregory VII and Innocent III in asserting and establishing the supremacy of the Papacy, but it was also largely instrumental in disrupting the feudal system which so generally determined the social, industrial, and political relations of men, and likewise powerfully augmented the hierarchical assumptions of the Roman Church. . . .

In France the process of centralizing royal power and of developing a genuine national state began with the Capetian kings. Philip Augustus (1180–1223) greatly extended the royal domain, chiefly at the expense of the English king, strengthened his control over all classes of his subjects, and at the same time by tactful concessions he increased his authority over the important towns. Philip's grandson, the heroic and popular Louis IX (1226–70), improved the government and greatly increased royal power by systemizing justice and taxation and by seeking the advice and assistance of a council made up of the powerful nobles and prelates. This body was divided into three sections: first, the king's council for aid in general matters; secondly, a chamber of accounts to look after the revenues; thirdly, the parliament to act as a supreme court with its seat fixed at Paris. It was left to his grandson Philip IV, called the Fair (1285–1314), first to play the role of an absolute monarch in France. To begin with he had inherited the best organized and best administered government the country had known up to that time. He surrounded himself with keen civil lawyers, who had derived their ideas of a monarch's prerogatives from a study of the Roman law and who encouraged Philip to gather up into his own hands the full reins of rule regardless of the privileges of his vassals and the clergy. Philip IV expelled the clergy from all participation in the administration of the law and made the lawyers supreme in the courts. They became, in consequence, the stoutest and ablest defenders of French political independence of the Papacy. Through these wise and efficacious means the decentralizing influences of feudalism were crushed and the foundations for the most powerful monarchy of Europe were laid.

With the development of royalty in

France also came a national consciousness, a common language, a common
tradition and history, and a common
patriotism which made France a strong
national state ready to support the king
in defending its rights against the pretensions and claims of the Pope.

From this brief survey of the new
political forces appearing in Europe in
the thirteenth century, it is apparent
that from three sources, at least, the assumptions of the Roman Papacy to universal temporal supremacy would not go
unquestioned. In the first place the
dawning consciousness of nationality
among the people of England, France,
Spain, and indeed even of Germany and
Italy, began to resent the extreme claims
of the Pope. In the second place, powerful
monarchs like the kings of England,
France, and Spain, and also the weaker
rulers in Germany and Italy, supported
by their subjects, were ready to assert
their political independence of Rome.
In the third place many educated lay
lawyers, imbued with the fundamentals
of the revised Roman law, were prepared
to supply the arguments which would
overthrow the claims of the head of the
Medieval Church to general secular
jurisdiction over Western Europe. The
opening years of the fourteenth century
were to witness a bold attack by these
forces upon Papal supremacy, which
greatly weakened its control. . . .

When the pious but weak and incapable old hermit Pope Celestine V, stag-
gered by the responsibilities of his high
office, abdicated the Papal throne in
1294, after four months of feeble rule,
to the joy of the cardinals and the sor-
row of the people of Rome, he was succeeded by Boniface VIII.

The pontificate of Boniface VIII marks
a notable epoch in the history of the
Latin Church. On his father's side he was

of Spanish origin, but through his mother
he represented an ancient family of
Roman counts which had given to the
Church Innocent IV, Gregory IX, and
Alexander IV. Born at Anagni, near
Rome, in 1221,[3] he studied civil and canon
law in Rome and probably at Paris, received his doctorate, and soon became a
recognized expert lawyer. It appears that
he served as a canon at Anagni, Todi,
Paris, and Rome, and about 1276 he became associated with the Roman Curia
and soon rose to prominence. In 1281,
at the age of 60, he was made cardinal
and represented the Papal See as legate
to France and England. His election as
Pope occurred at Naples on 24th December, 1294; but apparently it was not
popular with the Neapolitans, who seem
to have had little faith in him. Charles
II of Naples accompanied him to Rome,
where he was crowned with unusual
splendour. The kings of Naples and
Hungary walked by his side as, robed in
full pontificals and crowned, he rode
his white palfrey through the kneeling
crowds on his way to the Lateran accompanied by representatives of the
Roman nobility.

The inauguration of Boniface VIII
looked propitious, but troublous times
were ahead. He found the Papacy at the
height of its power; he died leaving it
humbled and weak. His ideals were as
lofty as those of Hildebrand; his ambitious pretensions to authority as great
as those of Innocent III. He stood con-
fidently on the ground tilled by the
former and sowed by the latter, but his
harvest was a failure. The causes for the
decline of Papal power during his pon-

---

[3] The date of Boniface's birth is actually uncertain.
1221 is deduced from unreliable chroniclers' reports
of his age at death, but an analysis of the chronology
of his career suggests that he was probably born
some fifteen years later.—*Ed.*

tificate are quite clear and easily explained.

1. Boniface was an old man on the verge of four-score years when elected. Although still very energetic, keen of intellect, and strong of will, yet he was woefully wanting in common courtesy, human tact, and a compromising spirit. He was overbearing, blunt, implacable, egotistic to an offensive degree, and possessed of a blind, insatiable thirst for power. He was deplorably lacking in wisdom and discernment. Indeed, a more unfortunate choice of Pope at this critical period could not have been made.

2. The times had changed—new forces had appeared in Europe to challenge the claims of the Papacy. These new forces could not be ignored, nor scolded away, nor even frightened into silence by Papal thunders and penalties. They had to be met and either destroyed or compromised with. Boniface, in his blindness, took no account of the new intellectual awakening of Europe. Apparently he was entirely unaware, likewise, of the significant social and industrial stirrings among the masses. He made no allowance for the new spirit of nationality showing itself in England, France, and elsewhere. He either stubbornly refused or else was impotent to gauge correctly the strength of the forces arrayed against him.

3. The open and disgraceful quarrel with Philip IV of France ended in the mortifying defeat of Boniface personally and in the weakening of the prestige held by the Papacy since the period of Gregory VII. Personal enemies made serious but in part groundless charges against his character and his faith. The French accused him of outright infidelity and even of denying the immortality of the soul. Dante, who visited Rome during his rule, denounced him as "the prince of modern pharisees," a usurper "who turned the Vatican hill into a common sewer of corruption," and assigned him a place in the lowest circles of hell. . . . He reigned for nine troubled years, but scarcely achieved a single decisive triumph. His pontificate marks the beginning of the decline of the power and glory of the Medieval Papacy.

Not the least of the problems associated with assessing the career of Boniface VIII is that of determining the facts. Historians hostile to his ambitions or to the papacy in general have seldom hesitated to paint his motives black, and those attempting to understand the true nature of his pontificate frequently find that their first task is to remove the overlay of innuendo and scandal that obscure it. Nowhere is this difficulty more apparent than in the treatment of the strange circumstances surrounding Celestine V's abdication and Boniface's succession, circumstances that were to haunt Boniface for the rest of his life. A classic example of the hostile school's approach is that of ADRIEN BAILLET (1649–1706), a *littérateur* of the age and circle of Louis XIV whose writings range from a life of Descartes to the work from which the following passage is taken. His point of view reflects that of his monarch, whose antipathy toward papal encroachments on royal sovereignty was well known.*

Adrien Baillet

Benedict Gaetani:
Ambitious Schemer

Philip the Fair, grandson of St. Louis, had been reigning for nine years in France when the Holy See, vacant because of the voluntary abdication of Pope Celestine V [December 13, 1294], was filled by Benedict Gaetani, who took the name Boniface VIII [December 24, 1294]. Celestine, known in private life as Pietro di Murrone, wished to preserve in his pontificate the holiness he had brought to it, but he found many obstacles in his path. As a result, love of his first monastic rule and of his former solitude[1]

joined with his lack of experience in the management of the Church's public affairs to make him listen willingly to the suggestions of certain people sent to him by those desirous of his office to exaggerate its dangers and obligations. To persuade a man so holy to resign, Boniface, the most impatient and adroit of those who sought to gain the Holy See, would have had no need for the artifices and ruses of which he has since been accused. He employed more than one of them, however, in his scheme to seduce

---

[1] Before his elevation to the papacy Celestine had been a hermit and a monk. He was the founder of a monastic order later known as the Celestines,

but his desire for the solitary life of holiness led him to depart from his followers. On this, see the selections by Hughes and Leclercq. —*Ed.*

---

*From Adrien Baillet, *Histoire des demeslez de Boniface VIII avec Philippe le Bel,* 2d edition (Paris, 1718), pp. 22–25. Translated by Charles T. Wood.

the simplicity of Celestine, whom he did not regard as a man of great force.

After having done everything possible to obtain Celestine's resignation, Boniface left no stone unturned to have himself elevated in his place. The methods he used to strengthen his hold on his new dignity were no better than the means he had employed to gain it. . . . Not content with having had his predecessor's abdication confirmed in the College of Cardinals and with having forced him to leave the city (after having himself expressed the wish to hear his confession in order to learn the secrets of his heart), he had him arrested on the pretext that someone might take advantage of his tractability to induce him to take up the idea of the papacy again, thus creating the threat of dangerous schism. Finally, judging that he would not be the peaceful possessor of the tiara so long as Celestine lived, with a cruelty that led all men of good will to express horror and aversion for his conduct, he forced him to end his days in a prison.

Boniface believed that he had removed the last obstacle to his ambition. Celestine's death seemed to leave those who refused to recognize him as legitimate pope without leader or pretext. Consequently, he no longer thought of anything but to carry out the plans he had made to gain for himself a temporal and spiritual sovereignty over every power in Christendom. . . .

PHILIP HUGHES (b. 1895) is a modern Catholic
historian whose multivolume works, *A History of the
Church* and *The Reformation in England,* have
received popular as well as scholarly praise. He is also
the author of numerous other books and articles on
ecclesiastical history. In treating the renunciation of
Celestine and the accession of Boniface, Hughes does
not disagree with Baillet's facts as much as he expands
upon them, giving fuller details. In so doing, however,
he arrives at a different interpretation, one that places
Boniface's motives and ambitions in rather a better
light.*

Philip Hughes

Benedict Gaetani:
The Church's Salvation

On Good Friday, 1292 (4 April), suddenly, unexpectedly, Nicholas IV died:
and in this great crisis of Christian history the cardinals left the Holy See vacant
for two and a quarter years.

The death of the pope brought the
whole crusade movement to a stand-
still. Whatever the latent enthusiasm of
the general body of the Christian people, the pope was the only sovereign
really anxious about the disaster; and
once it became evident that the twelve
cardinals[1] would be unable to make a
speedy election, the various princes
turned their attention to questions nearer
home.

The real centre of interest for the

Christian princes was the activities of
Philip the Fair . . . [who now] intervened to create a French party in Rome.
He found ready support in the Colonna
—that clan of Roman nobles who, for
centuries now, had played a leading
part in the politics of the papal state,
lords of a score of towns and fortresses
in the mountain country between Rome
and Naples, and masters thereby of the
communications between Rome and the
South; wealthy, ambitious and turbulent.
Their present head was that James
Colonna, . . . patron of the Franciscan
spirituals,[2] a cardinal since the time of

---

[1] Six Romans, four Italians, two French.

[2] The Spiritual Franciscans were a group of Friars
Minor who insisted on absolute poverty both for
themselves and for the order; many of them were

Nicholas III. In the late pope's reign he had been all powerful, and Nicholas IV, amongest other favours to the family, had created a second Colonna cardinal, Peter, the elder man's nephew. John Colonna, the older cardinal's brother had, in the same pontificate, ruled Rome for a time as senator.

James Colonna was, at this moment, one of six cardinals who remained in Rome, divided against their colleagues who had fled to Rieti from the plague, and divided still more bitterly among themselves into equal groups of pro-Colonna and pro-Orsini. The Colonna were the more powerful and had recently driven out the Orsini and it was to the Colonna cardinals that the French diplomacy now addressed itself, with offers of lands (September 1293).

In return the Colonna cardinals prepared to elect the kind of pope France wanted, and first they notified the absent majority of the Sacred College that they —the three who alone had remained in Rome—were the only real electors and that within a certain date they proposed to elect a pope. But this manoeuvre failed completely. All the train of canonists, Roman and foreign, whom the day to day business of the curia drew to Rome, was now at Rieti with the majority of the cardinals. The Colonna manifesto was put to them as a case in law. Unanimously they rejected the claim, and by five votes to two the Rieti cardinals made the decision their own, and fixed the coming feast of St. Luke (18 October, 1293) for the opening day of the conclave, the cardinals to assemble at Perugia. The Colonna had lost the first move, and the

appointed day found them reunited with their colleagues at Perugia.

The election, however, still continued to drag, and the factions remained deadlocked for yet another ten months. . . . Affairs had gone from bad to worse and seemed about to touch the worst itself, when, in the first week of July, the news arrived that the cardinals had elected a pope.

For the task of reconstructing the badly-damaged fabric of Christendom they had chosen an old man of eighty-five, Peter of Murrone, a hermit who, for many years now, had lived in the inaccessible solitudes of the Abruzzi. The newly elected had begun life as a Benedictine monk. After governing his monastery for a year as abbot, he had sought leave to live as a hermit. Soon the spiritual want of the peasantry around forced him into new activity as a kind of wandering preacher, and he became to this mountainous countryside very much what St. Francis had been, fifty years earlier, to Umbria. Disciples gathered round him and presently Peter had founded a new religious order which followed a way of life based on the rule of St. Benedict. And next, once the various houses of the order were established, the founder had given up his place in it, and had gone back to the life of solitude that had been his ideal throughout. What brought him to the notice of the cardinals in July 1294, was a letter one of them had received from him, violently denouncing their incapacity to provide the Church with a head, and threatening them all with the wrath of God unless they found a pope within four months. . . . The effect of the letter was instantaneous. That same day the cardinals chose Peter for pope (July 5, 1294).

Their choice, of course, struck the

---

strongly influenced by the apocalyptic writings of Joachim of Fiore. Though supported by Celestine V, they were later declared heretical by Boniface and John XXII.—*Ed.*

popular imagination immediately, as it has held it ever since. And yet the brief reign of Peter di Murrone was, as might have been expected, little short of disastrous. No one, in the end, realised this more clearly than Peter himself. There was only one way out of the situation, and being a saint he took it, abdicating his high office as simply as he had accepted it.

Peter was not enthroned as pope—and did not assume his papal name, Celestine V—until August 29, nine weeks after his election. The interval was filled with the beginnings of the great scandal that marked the reign. . . . The basis of this was, of course, the new pope's utter and absolute inexperience of anything beyond the guidance of a small community of peasant monks, his excessively delicate conscience, his simple belief in the goodness of man, and his never-ending desire to put all his authority and power into the hands of others while he retired to solitude and prayer. "His entire and dangerous simplicity" one chronicler of the time remarks as a cause of troubles, while another writes of his unawareness of frauds and of that human trickery in which courtiers excel.[3] In these brief weeks the papacy fell into the most complete servitude which, perhaps, it has ever endured; and it did so with the pope's entire good

---

[3] *Cf.* also the bull of his canonisation "And now, being of a marvellous simplicity and inexperienced in all that belongs to the ruling of the universal Church, as a man would be who from his earliest years down to extreme old age had shaped his heart to divine things and not to worldly matters . . . he yielded up the honour of being pope . . . lest, for the reasons given above, there might come upon the universal church, from his government of it, some catastrophe." *Qui Facit Magna* of Clement V (May 5, 1313) in Bullarium Romanum (edit. Cocquelines, Rome 1741, t. III pt 2 p. 142 § 12).

will, utterly unaware as he was of the consequences of his acts. . . .

Papal resources [were] shamefully exploited for the private profit of all who could get at the machinery; appointments, pensions, grants of land, of jurisdiction, of dispensations fell in showers. The pope was even induced to set his signature to blank bulls, which the recipient filled up as he chose. . . .

It had been a lifelong practice with Celestine to pass the whole of Lent and of Advent in absolute solitude and prayer, making ready for the great feasts of Easter and Our Lord's Nativity. Towards the end of November 1294, as Celestine began to speak of his coming retreat, the King [of Naples] suggested to him that, for the conduct of church affairs during these four weeks, it would be well to name a commission of three cardinals with full power to act in his name. Celestine agreed, but a cardinal (not one of the three) came across this extraordinary document as it awaited a final accrediting formality. He urged upon the pope that here was something beyond his powers. The Church, he said, could not have three husbands. And with this, Celestine's scruples began to master him. Quite evidently he was not the man for the office; ought he not to give it up? and after days of prayer and consultation with friends and with the canonists, he finally resolved the two questions that tormented his conscience. Could the lawfully-elected pope lawfully resign the office? How ought this to be done? The first point Celestine appears to have decided for himself on the general principles of resignation to be found in the manuals of Canon Law. The cardinals whom he consulted agreed that his view of the law was correct. In the delicate technical question about the best way to carry out his plan, Celestine had the expert assistance of Gerard Bianchi, cardinal-bishop of Sabina, and of Benedict Gaetani. Finally, he issued a bull declaring the pope's right to resign and then, in accordance with this, before the assembly of the cardinals, he gave up his great office, laying aside his mitre, his sandals and his ring (December 13, 1294).

Boniface VIII, 1294–1303

Celestine V had renewed the law of the conclave. This excellent measure brought it about that the vacancy was soon filled, for the election was over in a single day. At the first ballot Matteo Orsini was elected. He refused the office. The second ballot was inconclusive. At the third, the cardinals chose Benedict Gaetani, December 24, 1294. He took the name Boniface VIII.

Not the least of the difficulties that awaited whoever succeeded Celestine was the primary duty of neutralising the harm produced by the scandalous exploitation of the hermit pope's inexperience. And whatever the personal character and disposition of that successor, it would be only too easy to distort, for the generality of men, his restoration of the ordinary routine of a pope's life after the idyllic episode of Celestine—the pope who rode upon an ass to Aquila for his coronation, and who had lived in a hut of rough planking set up in the splendid hall of the royal palace at Naples.

Boniface VIII was not the man to be turned, for a moment, from his obvious duty by any such anxieties as these. Indeed—and this is one of the weaknesses in his character—it is doubtful if they would occur to him as causes for anxiety. He had a first-rate intelligence, highly trained, and a first-hand acquaintance

with every aspect of the complex problem before him, and with most of the leading personalities whom any attempt to solve it must involve. His own speciality was Law, and as papal jurist Boniface was to close, not unworthily, the great series of popes that began with Alexander III, just over a hundred years before him. He was himself the nephew of Alexander IV, and was thereby kin to the great Conti family whence had also come Innocent III and Gregory IX. For many years the various popes had made use of him in diplomatic missions, and one of these, in 1268, had brought him, in the suite of cardinal Ottoboni, to the London of Henry III, in the turbulent years that followed the Barons' War. The French pope, Martin IV, had created him a cardinal, and Boniface, in the Sacred College, seems to have been what, as pope, he described himself, always a strong friend to the interests of France and of Charles of Anjou. Certainly in his great mission to France in 1290[4]—the peak of his diplomatic career—he had not given signs of anything like a militant independence of the lay power as such. Indeed he had been all that was tactful and conciliatory towards Philip the Fair. In the conclave at Perugia he had shown himself amused and sceptical about the move to elect Celestine V, and for some time had kept aloof from the regime which followed. When finally he had rejoined his colleagues it had been to watch, somewhat disgusted, the uncontrolled plunder of rights and property that was the order of the day, and then, with his firm advice—once this was asked—to point the only way out of the scandal.

---

[4] This mission was connected with Philip the Fair's desire to end his father's crusade against Aragon, but while in France Cardinal Gaetani had also attempted to mediate disputes at the University of Paris, an intervention that caused hard feelings. —*Ed.*

Hostilities between France and the papacy began in February 1296 when BONIFACE VIII (1235?–1303) issued *Clericis laicos,* a bull that forbade laymen to tax the clergy. Since Philip the Fair and Edward I of England had both been accustomed to receive clerical subsidies with which to finance their wars, their reaction was understandably hostile and immediate. In studying *Clericis laicos,* the reader should consider not only the uncompromising style in which it is couched but also the nature of the political conceptions that underlie its arguments.*

Boniface VIII

Clericis Laicos

Boniface Bishop, servant of the servants of God, for the perpetual record of the matter. That laymen have been very hostile to the clergy antiquity relates; and it is clearly proved by the experiences of the present time. For not content with what is their own the laity strive for what is forbidden and loose the reins for things unlawful. Nor do they prudently realize that power over clerks or ecclesiastical persons or goods is forbidden them: they impose heavy burdens on the prelates of the churches and ecclesiastical persons regular and secular, and tax them, and impose collections: they exact and demand from the same the half, tithe, or twentieth, or any other portion or proportion of their revenues or goods; and in many ways they try to bring them into slavery, and subject them to their authority. And, we regret to say, some prelates of the churches and ecclesiastical persons, fearing where there should be no fear, seeking a temporary peace, fearing more to offend the temporal majesty than the eternal, acquiesce in such abuses, not so much rashly as improvidently, without obtaining authority or license from the Apostolic See. We therefore, desirous of preventing such wicked actions, decree, with apostolic authority and on the advice of our brethren, that any prelates and ecclesiastical persons, religious or secular, of whatsoever orders, condition or stand-

*From H. Be⸱⸱enson (ed. and trans.), *Documents of the Christian Church* (New York: Oxford University Press, 1947), pp. 159–161. Reprinted by permission of the Oxford University Press.

ing, who shall pay or promise or agree to pay to lay persons collections or taxes for the tithe, twentieth, or hundredth of their own rents, or goods, or those of the churches, or any other portion, proportion, or quantity of the same rents, or goods, at their own estimate or at the actual value, under the name of aid, loan, relief, subsidy, or gift, or by any other title, manner, or pretext demanded, without the authority of the same see. . . .

And also whatsoever emperors, kings, or princes, dukes, earls, or barons, powers, captains, or officials, or rectors, by whatsoever names they are called, of cities, castles, or any places whatsoever, wheresoever situate, and all others of whatsoever rank, eminence or state, who shall impose, exact, or receive the things aforesaid, or arrest, seize, or presume to take possession of things anywhere deposited in holy buildings, or to command them to be arrested, seized, or taken, or receive them when taken, seized, or arrested, and also all who knowingly give aid, counsel, or support, openly or secretly, in the things aforesaid, by this same should incur sentence of excommunication. Universities, too, which may have been to blame in these matters, we subject to ecclesiastical interdict.

The prelates and ecclesiastical persons above mentioned we strictly command, in virtue of their obedience, and on pain of deposition, that they in no wise ac-

quiesce in such things without express leave of the said see, and that they pay nothing under pretext of any obligation, promise, and acknowledgment whatsoever, made in the past, or in existence before this time, and before such constitution, prohibition, or order come to their notice, and that the seculars aforesaid do not in any wise receive it; and if the clergy do pay, or the laymen receive, let them fall under sentence of excommunication by the very deed.

Moreover, let no one be absolved from the aforesaid sentences of excommunications and interdict, save at the moment of death, without authority and special leave of the Apostolic See, since it is part of our intention that such a terrible abuse of secular powers should not be carried on under any pretense whatever, any privileges whatsoever notwithstanding, in whatsoever tenors, forms or modes, or arrangement of words, conceded to emperors, kings and the other aforesaid; and we will that aid be given by no one, and by no persons in any respect in contravention of these provisions.

Let it then be lawful to none at all to infringe this page of our constitution, prohibition, or order, or to gainsay it by any rash attempt; and if anyone presume to attempt this, let him know that he will incur the indignation of Almighty God, and of his blessed apostles Peter and Paul.

EDGAR BOUTARIC (1829–1877) was a nineteenth-century French medievalist whose primary interest was the rise of the Capetian dynasty, of which Philip the Fair was a member. In his short life he edited the *Actes du Parlement de Paris* and wrote such monographic studies as *Saint Louis et Alfonse de Poitiers* and *La France sous Philippe le Bel.* His history of Philip the Fair's reign was the first that made a genuine attempt to base its interpretations on official documents as well as on chroniclers' tales. While obviously French in his bias, Boutaric was not certain that the first encounter between Boniface and Philip could be understood in a purely Franco-papal context. As is apparent from the following account, he felt that the pope's unexpected humiliation was largely due to his entanglements in Italian affairs.*

Edgar Boutaric

The Importance of Italian Affairs

No events in the reign of Philip the Fair are more weighty or of higher interest than those marking his relations with the Holy See. His quarrel with Boniface VIII was to establish the limits of the popes' authority and keep it in just bounds, but this great enterprise [against the papacy] was accompanied by scandals and deplorable violence.

Until then Western Europe had formed a vast Christian republic of which the pope was supreme head. Rome had become mistress of the world. Never had the decrees of the Senate, supported by the victorious eagles of the legions, been more respected and feared than the bulls issued at the Vatican by the successor of St. Peter. The pope had been able with good reason to take over the motto of the Carolingian emperors: "Christ conquers, reigns, rules." Theocracy governed the world. Gregory VII [1073–1085] had begun this era of universal domination; his work was continued by his successors, particularly Honorious III [1216–1227] and Innocent IV [1243–1254]; but the ever increasing progress of monarchical power in each of the European states was beginning to obstruct these pretensions. More than once Philip Augustus [1180–1223] and St. Louis himself [1226–1270] resisted and demanded their independence.

Nevertheless, throughout the thirteenth century, the Holy See's right to intervene in the relations of princes

*From Edgar Boutaric, *La France sous Philippe le Bel* (Paris, Henri Plon, 1861), pp. 88–89, 92, 93, 94–99. Translated by Charles T. Wood. Footnotes omitted.

among themselves was universally recognized. Further, the sovereign pontiffs had numerous occasions on which to meddle in the internal government of the states of Europe. Natural protectors of the Church, they defended it against the encroachments of secular power; they exercised also a right of administration and control over the different national Churches. They intervened therefore at any given moment in the affairs of France to overrule the kings, to protect the Church and to govern it.

It is from this triple point of view that we will examine the relations of the papacy with Philip the Fair. . . .

Philip the Fair found only good will in Martin IV [1281–1285], Honorius IV [1285–1287], and Nicholas IV [1288–1292]. Nicholas IV was succeeded by Celestine V who, scarcely on the throne, voluntarily descended and was replaced by Cardinal Benedict Gaetani, who took the name Boniface VIII. He was an old man related to one of the first families of Italy, deeply versed in the science of civil and canon law; he was known for energy, pride, and an indomitable stubborness. His enemies supposed him to have limitless ambition and cupidity. He had met Philip the Fair personally during a stay in France as legate, and had been seized with affection for the young king. He later declared, on the eve of excommunicating him, that as a simple cardinal he had been French to the core, something that had often brought him reproaches from members of the sacred college. . . .

Boniface VIII met the fate reserved for the vanquished of this world; he succumbed, and everyone joined in condemning him. Frenchmen devoted to the monarchy, Gallicans jealous of their liberties, indifferent foreigners, skeptic philosophers, democratic writers, all have been unanimous in blaming and insulting

him. The contemporary chroniclers, even the ecclesiastical ones, did not spare him the historians of the Church have no dared to defend him. Gregory VII was called the Great, and Boniface VIII, his imitator, died in miserable circumstances leaving a dishonored memory! . . .

Boniface brought no new pretensions to the throne of St. Peter; his policy vis-à-vis foreign princes was that of his predecessors and strikingly resembles the project Sully attributed to Henry IV.[1] His avowed goal was the conquest of the Holy Land: he wished to re-establish peace among the Christian princes and turn their reunited arms against the Muslims. All who troubled the peace were in his eyes sacrilegious men who spilled the blood of the faithful and by their impious quarrels retarded the advent of the Church's domination over the entire universe.

It was with this great goal in mind that his predecessor Nicholas IV had bent every effort to re-establish good relations, underhandedly compromised, between Edward of England and Philip the Fair, and to prevent the hostilities that were not slow in breaking out. The capture of Saint-Jean-d'Acre in 1291 had had a sad and resounding echo in Europe. Boniface wanted to bring aid to the Holy Land, but the war involving France on one side and England and Flanders on the other tended to block his projects. He bent every effort to end it and proposed himself as mediator. A truce was concluded through his efforts. At the moment that it was about to expire (June 1297), he renewed it on his own authority and charged two cardi-

---

[1] A proposal by Henry IV of France (1589–1610) to establish a European "Christian Republic" based on a perpetual peace guaranteed by an alliance system among the various states, and complete with a supranational senate or general council.—*Ed.*

nals, the bishops of Albano and Palestrina, with informing Philip the Fair.

Philip refused to listen to the reading of the pontifical bull before making the following protest: That the temporal government of his kingdom pertained to him alone; that he did not recognize any superior in this matter; that he would never submit to any living soul in this regard; that he wished to exercise his jurisdiction in his fiefs, defend his kingdom, and pursue his rights with the aid of his subjects, his allies, and God; that the truce did not bind him. As for spiritual matters, he was inclined, following the example of his predecessors, humbly to receive the warnings of the Holy See as a true son of the Church.

Philip accepted the mediation of Boniface not as pope but as a private person: he obtained from the pontiff a bull in which Boniface bound himself to pronounce arbitral judgment only in his capacity as Benedict Gaetani and only after having received letters patent from the king giving approval to his decision. This conduct of Philip the Fair must have given pause to Boniface and made him realize the need to deal carefully with a prince who was so jealous of his authority and who repulsed the intervention of the successor of St. Peter, before whom kings up to then had bowed. Boniface knew how to make trouble and also how to contain himself for a while, but the relations between the king and the pope were too frequent for these haughty and dominating individuals not to clash violently in the end.

In 1296, a group of the clergy of France brought complaints to the Holy See against what it called the exactions of Philip the Fair, and these were much more favorably received than were similar complaints from England, where Edward was employing much more energetic methods than his rival to obtain subsidies from the clergy. The occasion was right for Boniface; he did not pass it up. The bull *Clericis laicos* (1296, with no month given, but before August 18), which excommunicated both those who levied imposts on the clergy and the ecclesiastics who paid them, was applicable to the whole Christian world. Issued in a moment of irritation, it was too exaggerated to be enforced. Boniface had gone too far, and he understood this. . . . The bull *Ineffabilis amor* corrected what its predecessor had made too absolute. Philip could levy subsidies on the clergy, with the consent of the pope, who, if the kingdom was threatened, would order contributions for its defense up to the sale of sacred vessels. Boniface asked in the same bull for an explanation of the prohibition recently placed by Philip on the export of gold, silver, and merchandise from the kingdom, a prohibition that threatened to cut off one of the principal revenues of Rome.

The royal edict that is unanimously represented as Philip's reply to the bull *Clericis laicos* was not directed against the pope, as it was issued in April, a few days after the drawing up of the bull and before there was time for it to have become known to the king of France. The edict did not apply solely to money; it included prohibitions against the export of arms, horses, and other objects. It was intended to hit the English and the Flemings, with whom the French were at war; similar edicts were promulgated in Philip's reign on many occasions.

In the bull *Ineffabilis amor,* Boniface threatened Philip with excommunication; he presented him as hated by his subjects and surrounded by enemies who were awaiting only the right moment to invade his kingdom. What would become of him if he lost the favor of the Holy See, which had sustained him till then (September 21, 1296)? Philip and his counselors were indignant over the liberty that Boniface was taking and resolved to rebuff his imperious warnings, which belonged to a previous era. Dupuy[2] has published a response that was, it is claimed, sent to Rome, but the indecency of its tone suffices to show that it was never sent. It is nothing more than a memorandum presented to the king by some courtier, and never even finished, as the title on the sole known contemporary example attests, a title that Dupuy suppressed, substituting one of his own making.

The king gave satisfactory explanations. In 1297, new prohibitions against exporting gold and silver, new alarms from the pope, new threats, new explanations from Philip. In the meantime the bishops of France wrote to Boniface VIII asking him to grant the king a tithe on the churches. The clergy understood that it could not keep from contributing to the defense of the country. The letter contrasts singularly with a protest made by the monastery of Cîteaux, a protest directed no less against the bishops than against the king. The hostility of the monks to the bishops had long been successful, thanks to the help of the pope, who found faithful tools in the regulars, but the time was coming when monks, bishops, and pope were going to bow before the royal power.

Abandoned by a part of the Gallican clergy, Boniface made new concessions. By the bull *Romana mater ecclesia* he even permitted the levying, in cases of necessity, of ecclesiastical tithes without the consent of the Holy See, but with that of the clergy. The bull *Noveritis nos* went further. It left to the king, if he were of age, and to his council, if he were a minor, the decision as to whether there was necessity or not, and the right to impose ecclesiastic tithes, even without consulting the pope. It ended by declaring that the Holy See had never intended to diminish the rights, liberties, franchises, and customs of the kingdom, of the king, and of the barons. The pope even wrote to the prelates of the province of Reims that he was prepared to consecrate the goods of the Roman Church and his own person to the defense of the kingdom.

This compliance of Boniface VIII, this sudden meekness, must not be attributed entirely to feelings of good will toward Philip the Fair: it is explained primarily by the difficult situation in which the pope found himself in his own States.

Boniface belonged by family to the Ghibelline party; as pope, he became Guelf.[3] As cardinal, he had the Colonnas for enemies, heads of the emperors' party. Nevertheless the Colonnas and the Orsinis had combined to make the choice fall on Benedict Gaetani at the conclave called to pick a successor to Celestine V. Boniface appears to have forgotten this service: he left the Colonnas in the lurch and in no way let them participate in the favors of the new reign. They felt resentment toward Boniface for his ingratitude, and the feeling was intensified when one of them [Sciarra] believed Boniface had injured him in intervening in his domestic affairs. To avenge himself,

---

[2] Pierre Dupuy's *Histoire du differend d'entre le pape Boniface VIII et Philippes le Bel, roy de France* (Paris, 1655) is a monumental folio volume that prints nearly all the extant documents and chronicles concerning the affair.—*Ed.*

[3] The Ghibellines and the Guelfs were the two principal political factions in Italy, the former generally supporting the German Empire, the latter the papacy.—*Ed.*

Sciarra attacked the pontifical treasure on the road from Anagni and seized it. Two cardinals of the Colonna family withdrew into castles, where they plotted with the enemies of the pope: Boniface summoned them to remit to him those castles which threatened his safety. They refused and, basing their position on the renunciation of Celestine, denied the legitimacy of Boniface's election. Cited to Rome so that they might be placed under the necessity of recognizing him as pope, they did not present themselves. They were deprived of their dignities, and they and their relatives and supporters were excommunicated to the fourth generation, and then their goods were confiscated. Boniface, exceeding all limits of hate, extended the anathema to all those who might give asylum to these unfortunates, and struck with an interdict the places where they might seek a refuge against his pitiless anger. He preached a crusade against their partisans. The Ghibellines were defeated, their estates taken, and Palestrina, where the two Colonna cardinals had sought shelter, received a terrible punishment:

Boniface had it leveled. The ground it had occupied was put to the plow and sown with salt to dedicate it to sterility; a single church was left standing, attesting to the kind of vengeance Boniface VIII wrought on those who dared resist him (1299). But three years were needed for him to obtain this triumph. That is why in 1297, at the height of his quarrel with the Colonnas, Boniface withdrew the bull *Clericis laicos* and made peace with Philip the Fair. He did this so that he could dedicate himself completely to the annihilation of the Ghibelline party in the States of the Church.

Modern historians looking for the causes of the dispute between Boniface and Philip the Fair have often been mistaken. For most of them the enmity of the king toward the pope originated with the bull *Clericis laicos*. The facts prove that after the bull the accord between the two courts, troubled for a moment, was greater than ever. The pope on his own initiative granted a tithe and a year's revenue of the benefices that had become vacant in France during the course of the war. . . .

In the early decades of the present century the dominant French medievalist was CHARLES-VICTOR LANGLOIS (1863–1929); so unquestioned were his judgments that he was often, though not to his face, referred to as "the king of France." He wrote widely on medieval social and cultural history and was the editor of *Histoire littéraire de la France*. His best-known political works are *Le règne de Philippe III, le Hardi* and the volume on the period 1226–1328 in Ernest Lavisse's monumental *Histoire de France,* from which the present selections are taken. Although Langlois was well aware of Boutaric's interpretation of the first quarrel between Boniface and Philip, he developed a different view: Italian affairs *were* important, perhaps, but only because Philip was able to manipulate them cleverly to gain his own ends.*

Charles-Victor Langlois

The Power Politics of France

The first quarrel between Philip and Boniface lasted scarcely a year. The king's victory was prompt and decisive.

The extraordinary taxes, or tithes, imposed on the clergy of France which the popes had granted Philip III and Philip IV were, in theory, for support of the crusade—the crusade against Aragon[1]— that is, a war against a neighboring kingdom. The kings had thus become accustomed to counting on the ecclesiastical tax for their war expenses.

Although peace was restored between France and Aragon at the Congress of Anagni in 1295, war began in 1294 between France and England. The royal government wanted the subsidies from the clergy which it had had at its disposal against Aragon for use against England. Some provincial synods, convoked by its orders, voted for a tithe for two years, beginning with All Saints [November 1], 1294. They voted for it, but not without a recalcitrant minority protesting to Rome; the majority, in certain provinces—at Aurillac, for example —made it contingent upon the pope's assent, *salvo in his nostri summi pontificis beneplacito voluntario,* "unless the needs of the kingdom were so urgent

---

[1] The Aragonese had supported and taken over the Sicilian Vespers, a successful revolt in 1282 against Charles of Anjou, king of Sicily and brother of Louis IX of France. The French crusade against Aragon (1285 on), strongly supported by the pope, had stemmed from this incident.—*Ed.*

---

*From Charles-Victor Langlois, *Saint Louis—Philippe le Bel: Les derniers Capétiens directs,* volume III[2] of Ernest Lavisse, *Histoire de France* (Paris, 1902), pp. 131–139. Reprinted by permission of Librairie Hachette et Cie., Paris. Translated by Charles T. Wood. Some footnotes omitted.

that one could not wait for it without great danger." In 1296, there was a new vote, by an assembly of prelates, for imposition of a tax on clerics, and again new recriminations. This time, the complaints that the [Cistercian] Order of Cîteaux brought to the attention of the pope were emphatic: the king was compared with Pharaoh, the servile bishops who agreed to the taxes at the bidding of the king's men, with the "mute dogs" of Scripture. In a similar case twenty-eight years earlier, Clement IV had been content to rebuff those who complained. But Boniface hurled the celebrated bull that opened hostilities.

The bull *Clericis laicos* of February 24, 1296, forbade in general terms, under pain of excommunication, all secular princes from demanding or receiving extraordinary subsidies *(collectae, talliae)* from the clergy, and forbade the clergy to pay such subsidies unless they received authorization to do so from the apostolic see. This doctrine was not new: it had been affirmed by the [Fourth] Lateran Council (in the time of Philip Augustus) and by the canonist Guillaume Durand in his *Speculum judiciale;* even the affirmation of the traditional hostility between clerics and laymen that appears at the opening of the bull of February 24, 1296, *Clericis laicos infestos oppido tradit antiquitas,* is taken from the *Decretals* of Gratian.[2] But Boniface, with a new inflexibility, claimed certain powers that had hitherto received only tacit consent.

Neither Philip nor Edward of England, equally affected by *Clericis laicos,* acquiesced.

In France, an assembly of the clergy was convoked [by the king] to deliberate on the bull, and the assembly delegated the bishops of Nevers and Béziers to discuss it at Rome.[3] Further, a royal ordinance of August 17 forbade the export of gold and silver from the kingdom and, in addition, forbade Italian bankers in France from accepting payments to the account of the pope and of the cardinals.

The pope did not wait for this riposte. Before having received the envoys of the French clergy and news of the ordinance of August 17, he wrote the king many very friendly letters, as though he were no longer thinking of the February bull. Such was his cast of mind that he never suspected, it seems, what sort of impression the trenchant tone of his manifestoes was producing beyond the Alps. When he was informed of it, he drew up, on September 20, a very lively rejoinder. This is the bull that begins, *Ineffabilis amor.* The ordinance of August 17 is described in it as absurd, tyrannical, senseless: "Has someone wished to strike out at the pope and the cardinals, his brothers? What! to place audacious hands on those who depend on no secular power!" The pope reminded Philip that he (the king) had ruined the spirit of his own subjects, while he, Boniface, had spent sleepless nights because of his concern for France: "Look at the kings of the Romans, of England, of the Spains, who are thy enemies; thou hast attacked them, the injured parties. Wretch! do not forget that without the support of the Church thou

---

[2] "Antiquity informs us that laymen have greatly oppressed the clergy." Gratian's *Decretals* were a leading twelfth-century compilation of Canon Law. —*Ed.*

[3] For their part, the archbishop of Reims and his suffragans, apparently alarmed by the audacity of the pontiff and concerned about the consequences, wrote to Boniface to draw his attention to probable reprisals: "The king and his barons," they wrote, "reproach us for not contributing to the defense of the kingdom, although prelates are held to do so, some by the obligation of their fiefs, almost all by the oath of fealty; the king threatens us with withdrawal of the support we need in order to live in safety; this is the ruin of the Church. . . . "

canst not resist them. What would happen to thee, were thou to make her the ally of thy enemies, and thy principal adversary?"

Then proceeding to an interpretation of the bull *Clericis laicos,* Boniface said that it had been barbarized by the insolence of the king's counselors, and he explained it in these terms: "We have not declared, my dear son, that the clerics of thy kingdom cannot grant thee money subsidies in the future for the defense of thy kingdom, *pro defensione regni tui,* but only that, thanks to the excesses committed by thy officials, such levies cannot be made without our permission. I know that there are malevolent people around thee who insinuate: 'Prelates are no longer going to be able to serve the king with their fiefs; they shall no longer be able to give him even a cup or a horse.' This is false! We have explained this many times in conversation with thy counselors." Boniface then ended by begging the king to listen to the bishop of Viviers, his legate, who would explain the pontiff's thought to him in detail.

The explanations of the bishop of Viviers will never be known, nor what was said in the conversations between Boniface and the counselors of the king at Rome. But the indignation the letter *Ineffabilis* stirred up in the French court was expressed in many anonymous pamphlets appearing in 1296, the first specimens of antipapal literature in the reign of Philip the Fair. Perhaps the most interesting is the "Dialogue Between a Cleric and a Knight," in which the principle of the royal tax on ecclesiastical goods "for the defense of the kingdom" is sharply posed and justified by some very strong arguments: "Ecclesiastical immunity, granted by the charters of princes, can be revoked or suspended by the princes in the public interest. And let no one say that the right of revocation belongs only to the emperor, not to kings; the king of France has the right to modify imperial legislation; he is above the laws."

The most famous of the pamphlets, which was copied into a register of the royal archives, begins without salutation, in this manner: *"Antequam essent clerici, rex Franciae habebat custodiam regni sui."* It must not be believed, as it has been held in the past, that this reply to the letter *Ineffabilis* was sent to the pope under the seal of the king of France. It is a proposal for a reply that was doubtless never dispatched, but the letter, with its solemn and icy style—though without insults—is nonetheless remarkable.

"Before there were clerics," begins the anonymous author—who is familiar with the circulars of Frederick II[4]—"the kings of France had charge of this kingdom and the right to legislate for its security. Hence, the ordinance of the month of August. . . . Holy Mother Church, the bride of Christ, is not composed solely of priests; laymen are also a part of it; it is not for clerics alone that Christ is risen from the dead. . . . Clerics must contribute, like everyone else, to the defense of the kingdom; in this their interests are no different from those of laymen, for the foreigner, if he were the conqueror, would handle them no differently. . . . Is it not astonishing that the vicar of Jesus Christ may forbid paying tribute to Caesar and fulminate anathema against the clergy, who, as useful members of society, may aid the king, the kingdom, and themselves in proportion to their strength? To give money to jugglers and to their friends

---

[4] The emperor Frederick II in the 1240s had circulated many pamphlets of similar phraseology against Pope Innocent IV.—*Ed.*

according to the flesh, to squander money excessively on robes, cavalcades, banquets, and other secular pomp, such things clerics are permitted. But if illicit things are allowed, here is a case where the licit is forbidden. To think that clerics have been fattened . . . with the liberalities of princes, and yet should not aid them in their needs! But this would be to aid the enemy, to bring upon themselves the accusation of high treason, to betray the defender of the commonwealth!" Then the king, who supposedly speaks at this point, examines Boniface's observations about his foreign policy: he says that he honors God, the Catholic Church, its ministers, following the example of his ancestors, but he is disdainful of threats, for his rights make his position strong. Besides, the Church owes more to him and his house than to anyone else; she would be wrong to prove ungrateful. . . . Such was the stand a legist at the court of France would have liked to see Philip take beyond the one he actually took.[5]

In spite of the outburst of anger [stirred up by the letter *Ineffabilis*] of which

---

[5] It was at about this time that Pierre de Paroi, the prior of La Chaise and a secret agent of Philip the Fair, who from 1295 may have been conferring with Hugh Aicilin and the Colonnas, Boniface's enemies in the Sacred College, would for the first time have heard talk of the "errors, horrors and heresies" of the pope. The king of France, when he heard this, may have begged him to tell Boniface of the rumors circulating about him. Pierre de Paroi later said that he actually attempted to carry out this unlikely mission. "Who told thee that?" Boniface is said to have asked. "I named Philip, the son of the count of Artois, and my lord Jacques of Saint-Pol, since he could take no action against them." He shouted, "These knights are drunkards who are getting mixed up in things that do not concern them. What a perfect example of the overbearing pride of the French. Get out, debauched and false monk. May God confound me if I do not confound the overbearing pride of the French. I shall destroy the Colonnas. I shall dethrone the king of France. Every other Christian king will be with me against him."

Boniface was doubtless aware, the surprising thing at first sight, but a fact, is that this time he was not obstinate. We read in the bull *Romana Mater* of February 7, 1297: "Whenever an ecclesiastic of thy kingdom shall have voluntarily granted thee a contribution, we authorize thee to collect it, in cases of pressing need, without recourse to the Holy See." In this document Boniface repeated the reproaches contained in the letter *Ineffabilis* about the prohibition of August 17, which he had taken strongly to heart, but with some temperance and hints of compromise. He had yielded, and in the course of the year 1297 his chancery dispatched bull after bull giving the king of France complete satisfaction.

On February 1, [1297], the prelates of France, again assembled at Paris, wrote to the court of Rome that the recent treason of the count of Flanders, who had just become allied with the king of England, created an exceptional situation: "The king and his barons have asked the prelates and everyone in the kingdom to contribute toward the common defense. In the judgment of many, the recent bull *(Clericis laicos)* does not apply in the event of an urgent need. The king, our lord, is animated by such a respect for the Roman Church that, in spite of everything that could be suggested to him, he let nothing be done against the said bull, even though he knew that in England and elsewhere no one has paid any attention to it. We beg you quickly to grant us permission to furnish the king the subvention he asks, for we have reason to fear that the distress of the kingdom and, among some, evil intentions may push laymen into pillaging the goods of the churches if we do not join with them in the common defense." On the 28th, the pope, once more protesting his particular solicitude for France, granted the desired authorization. On March 7 he ordered the order of Cîteaux to give in. Finally, in July he capitulated completely: in letters addressed to the clergy, nobility, and people of France, he surrendered to the king, if of age, and to the royal council, in cases of minority, the function of sovereign decision as to when there was "need" and, consequently, the right to decide whether the pope needed to be consulted for levies of tithes agreed to by the prelates. The bull *Etsi de statu* of July 31 contained formal renunciation of the authority to defend ecclesiastical goods against the arbitrary will of kings, claimed in *Clericis laicos.*

This was a complete victory for the royalist position. It was accompanied by spiritual and temporal favors from Rome which were showered upon Philip and his counselors, who had been so harshly stigmatized a short time before. Philip received half of the bequests made in the previous ten years for the aid of the Holy Land, the first year's revenues from vacant benefices, etc. Boniface, who informed the king of the state of his health and affectionately recalled his stay in Paris, solemnly pronounced the canonization of St. Louis in the month of August; he permitted Philip to bar from office those clerics who might betray "the secrets of the kingdom of France, who might seek to do him harm, and who might foment troubles"; he delegated to the archbishop of Narbonne and the bishops of Dol and Auxerre the power to create, in the king's name, a canon in every cathedral and collegiate church of France. To "our dear son, the noble Pierre Flote, counselor of our very dear son Philip," he granted "for his merits" the lucrative right to confer titles of notary public in the name of the apostolic authority.

The pope, beaten in France, beaten in England (where *Clericis laicos* had no more success than on the Continent), underwent still further humiliations. Following the example of his predecessors, who had often been appointed arbiters of disputes among Christians, he had busied himself re-establishing peace between France and England. But Philip accepted his intervention only with reservations. On April 20, 1297, at Creil, the cardinals of Albano and of Preneste appeared at the French court: Boniface had decided to force the two warring kings to conclude a truce under his auspices until midsummer 1298.

Before allowing the legates to read the pontifical letters, Philip had it expressly declared that "the government of the kingdom belongs to the king, and to him alone; that he recognizes no superior; that he owes submission to no living man for temporal things." In June 1298, the representatives of the king of France accepted the arbitration of Boniface only on condition that the said Boniface would act in this event not as sovereign pontiff but as a private person, as "Benedict Gaetani." To add insult to injury, although the French in no ways treated him with respect, Boniface was forced to allow them to take precedence over the curia for several years, beginning in the summer of 1297. That his mind was made up to please them during this period was evident. The arbitral judgment he pronounced in 1298 was very partial, in their favor: "Sire," wrote an envoy of the count of Flanders from Italy in February 1299, "the king (of France) has so perverted the court that only with difficulty can someone be found who dares openly to speak of him in terms other than praises. . . . "

This extreme compliance of a pope so proud, this entente cordiale, prolonged for several years after a signal check, is to be explained by the financial and political embarrassment of the Holy See.

At that time Boniface was deeply engaged in the hornets' nest of Italian politics. . . . The Colonna family, powerful in the old land of the Hernici, allies of the Contis in the Roman Compagna, of the Annibaldis in the maritime districts, of the lords from the neighborhood of Anagni, Alatri, and Ferentino, was represented in the Sacred College, at the accession of Boniface VIII, by James and Peter Colonna, uncle and nephew. These cardinals, favorites of Nicholas IV and Celestine V, had, like the Orsinis, voted for Benedict in 1294: the Gaetanis were their dependents. But Boniface made it known that all the favors granted by Celestine would be reviewed, and he reserved his own for the people of Todi and Anagni, and for his own family, which was overwhelmed with them at the expense of the Colonnas. A vendetta ensued. . . .

On May 2, Stephen Colonna, brother of the cardinal Peter, placed himself in ambush on the Appian Way, seized the pontifical treasure being brought from Anagni to Rome . . . , and brought it to the castle of Palestrina. Some days later, Boniface addressed the people of Rome, gathered at the porch of St. Peter's, haranguing against the race of the Colonnas. "The Church," he said, "has fattened their insolence. What a crime is theirs! . . . Violence has been done to the pope. What are you waiting for? As God is our witness, we do not regret the stolen money, but if we stretch our patience, or rather our negligence, to the point of letting such a scandal go unpunished, who shall hesitate to say: 'You pretend to judge kings and yet dare not attack a few vermin!'" He recalled the crimes of

the two cardinals: "Peter has been the head of the Ghibellines and of the persecutors of the Church. . . . It was Cardinal James who prolonged the vacancy of the Holy See at Perugia for such a long time, a circumstance that caused disorder and numberless murders. Both have occupied and taken from the Roman Church lands that belong to her. Pride has caused their fall, like that of the sinful angels, and their fall will teach them that the Roman pontiff, whose name is known throughout the world, is alone superior to all."

On their side, the Colonna cardinals drew up a manifesto that they dated from the castle of Longhezza: "Benedict Gaetani," they said, "who pretends to be Roman pontiff, shouted the other day: 'At the end, I want to know whether I am the pope, yes or no.' On this point, we are in a position to reply. No, you are not the legitimate pope, and we beg the Sacred College to bring counsel and remedy to this irregularity." Celestine V did not have the right to abdicate. "We must work for the convocation of a council which will be able to provide for the salvation of the Church, threatened by the usurpations of a tyrant." On the day of the Ascension (May 23), Boniface's judgment was published, with the approval of the Sacred College: the two cardinals were deposed as schismatics and blasphemers; their goods, and those of Agapit, Stephen, and James, called *Sciarra*, sons of John Colonna, were confiscated; all were excommunicated and placed under the ban of Christianity.

For Boniface, who had so haughtily posed the principle of the Church's sovereignty over all peoples in the preamble to the bull *Ineffabilis amor,* imposing the Church's will by force on the Colonna family was a difficult task. . . . In June, the Colonnas sent a justificatory memorandum on their conduct to the University of Paris, whose professors, still suffering from the impact of a virulent speech that Benedict Gaetani as legate had bestowed upon them in 1290, had just drawn up an advisory opinion on the case of Celestine. Thomas of Montenero, archdeacon of Rouen, was charged with pointing out to the king of France that the Colonnas had acted in accordance with the advice of the masters of Paris; it was in defending the honor of the king against Boniface that the two cardinals had become worthy of his hate. This emissary encountered in Tuscany, as if by chance, a French mission that was going to Rome. Pierre Flote, head of the mission, let it be understood by the Colonnas' man that the king himself was also about to declare himself against Boniface.

The news soon spread; Boniface was informed; Pierre Flote was actually counting on it. The pope's fear that an alliance between Philip and the Colonnas was becoming immediate doubtless led him to welcome the envoys and the demands of the king of France with particular eagerness. Pierre Flote thus used a kind of extortion to swindle the pope into granting the canonization of St. Louis, the bull *Etsi de statu,* and all the other letters dated in July and August that he brought back to France from Orvieto. As for the Colonnas, they were abandoned. . . . Toward the end of the year Boniface granted those who took up the cross against the Colonnas the same indulgences as were granted to those who left for the Holy Land.

The Colonnas submitted in the fall of 1298. But fear of an alliance of the king of France with the Colonnas and the supporters of Celestine was not the only reason for Boniface's attitude. The war against the Aragonese and Ghibellines of Sicily, which was being carried on at the Holy See's expense, had not ended. On October 1, 1298, the pope asked the bishop of Vienne to seek subsidies for him from the clergy of France. "This is," he said, "the price for re-establishing the Church's authority in Sicily, a necessary condition for a crusade overseas." In short, during the last years of the thirteenth century, the court of France influenced Boniface either by the threat of a pact with his domestic enemies, or by monetary services; and beyond the Apennines the pope simply lacked the spare time to take on the airs of an irritated master which were, one day, to cost him dear.

In their first encounter Boniface VIII and Philip the Fair both showed their awareness of the difficulties the pope faced, thanks to the strange circumstances of his accession. The nature of these difficulties is nowhere better illustrated than in the following document issued by the condemned cardinals JAMES and PETER COLONNA in June 1297. Couched as an appeal to the University of Paris, this manifesto should be considered not only as a condemnation by some of Boniface's more violent enemies, but also as a statement which may reflect more widespread, and less prejudiced, concern about the pope's legitimacy.*

James and Peter Colonna

Third Manifesto Against Boniface VIII

James of S. Maria in Via Lata and Peter of S. Eustachio, by the mercy of God cardinal deacons, to the venerable chancellor and the venerable college of masters and scholars of the university of Paris, greetings and sincere love in the Lord.

Hear the voice of our prayer, we beseech you, O cultivators of justice, masters and disciples of the truth, that you, together with the kings and princes and peoples of the world, may weigh accurately in the balance of your judgement with the truth accompanying your decision the justice of our cause or rather that of the spouse of Christ and the iniquity of Benedict Gaetani, no bishop of the universal church but a tyrant, who holds the Roman church that he has

occupied only by an iniquitous act. . . . By evil advice and false arguments he and his accomplices persuaded our lord pope Celestine V of happy memory to renounce the apostolic office, though this was contrary to the rules and statutes of divine, human and canon law and a cause of scandal and error to the whole world. Then, when Celestine had resigned the papacy *de facto*—for he could not do so *de iure* since it is clear to all who are willing to investigate the matter carefully that the Roman pope cannot resign or give up the papacy or be released from it except by God alone—he did not fear to put himself *de facto* since he could not do it *de iure* in the place of the same lord Celestine who was still

*Brian Tierney, *The Crisis of Church & State 1050–1300*, © 1964. Reprinted by permission of Prentice-Hall, Inc., Englewood Cliffs, New Jersey. Pp. 176–178.

alive, and this under the eyes of our-selves and the other cardinals then present who were deceived by the suddenness of such an unheard-of act. . . . Conscious of the evil origin of his dignity and fearing the truth he savagely pursued the above-mentioned holy man [Celestine] who sought in every way to escape his tyranny, and when he had finally captured him cruelly imprisoned him at the castle of Fumone in the Campagna, which is not far from Anagni, and there caused him to die miserably. . . .

Who could be silent about such things with a clear conscience, when we saw the state of the church and the honor due to prelates constantly diminished. For he summoned to appear personally prelates from the most remote parts of the world whom he believed to be wealthy, not only to extort money from them but to strip them altogether, and this on pain of deprivation which they incurred automatically if they did not obey, and without even a pretended reason let alone a true one. As soon as he heard that churches were vacant he reserved the appointments to the judgement of his own disordered will, forbidding the electors to exercise their right of election and, what is more revolting, he did this in the case of many cathedral churches while their prelates were still alive. . . . It was as though, conscious of his evil conduct and always fearful of falling from his dignity, he wanted to institute prelates everywhere throughout the world by his own hand so that, when the question of his illegal entry was raised, they would not dare to speak against him, being afraid for their own positions. . . . And so in his time the church has become corrupt. No one re-ceives any favor without handing over a gift.

Again, even a true pontiff is accustomed and even bound to seek the advice of the cardinals and to obtain their consent in certain arduous affairs, especially in alienating the goods of the church, but this pseudo-pontiff does not deign to seek their counsel or await their consent. Rather if we or any of our brothers put forward any word that is contrary to his own opinion, he attacks the speaker with scathing words and, boasting that he rules over kings and kingdoms even in temporal affairs, he does not fear to assert that he can do anything of his own will by virtue of his plentitude of power, although no legitimate papal authority inheres in him. . . .

Consider then with faithful discernment God and his holy church so that, when the illegitimate usurper has been deposed and cast out, a true and legitimate pastor may rule truly, legitimately and canonically over the church his mother, the bride of Christ, redeemed by the blood of her spouse. Lest the sacraments of the church be further profaned, let all the acts of the same Benedict be suspended since he has been justly denounced by us, and let care be taken that a universal council be swiftly assembled which, laying aside all error, will declare the truth concerning the iniquity, nullity and injustice of the process he has presumed to institute against us. And meanwhile let no one obey or heed, especially in matters touching the safety of the soul, this man who does not possess the authority of a supreme pontiff although *de facto* he rashly holds the place of one.

The discussion in the selection from Langlois implies that Philip the Fair found his hand strengthened in his first quarrel with Boniface by the willingness of the University of Paris to find Celestine's renunciation and Boniface's election invalid, but what was the true opinion of the theologians? This is a question JEAN LECLERCQ (b. 1911) attempts to answer, and his views may help to explain the future course of the controversy. Leclercq is a French Benedictine who has written many books and articles on ecclesiastical matters. He is probably best known to English-speaking readers for his *Love of Learning and the Desire for God,* a study of monastic culture during the Middle Ages.*

Jean Leclercq

The Legitimacy of Boniface VIII

Following the death of Nicholas IV on April 4, 1292, the Holy See was vacant for two years due to the inability of the cardinals to agree on a new pope. On July 5, 1294, the eleven cardinals met in conclave at Perugia and unanimously elected Pietro di Murrone, who took the name Celestine V. A hermit of great purity of life, he had excelled in communicating his zeal for the austere life to the disciples he had gathered together, organized as a religious order, and who were later to take the name of Celestines. He was less skillfull in governing the Church, especially at a time when the rebel Spirituals were engendering in men's spirits a dangerous headiness that politicians endeavored to exploit in the service of their various interests.

The cardinals soon perceived the error they had made, and the question began to be posed in the Sacred College of the possibility of Celestine V's renouncing the pontifical throne. Precedents were sought in canonical tradition. Those found were of legendary origin, but at least they were believed to be authentic, and they did suffice to make people envisage the renunciation as possible. Cardinal Benedict Gaetani had acquired a growing influence over Celestine's thinking: he was charged with preparing him for this denouement. After

*From Jean Leclercq, "La Renonciation de Célestin V et l'opinion théologique en France du vivant de Boniface VIII," *Revue d'histoire de l'Eglise de France,* XXV (1939), pp. 183–186, 188, 189–192. Reprinted by permission of Dom Jean Leclercq, Abbaye Saint-Maurice, Clervaux, Luxemburg. Translated by Charles T. Wood. Footnotes omitted.

some hesitation Celestine V renounced the sovereign pontificate on December 13, 1294, and on December 24 Cardinal Benedict Gaetani was elected to succeed him under the name of Boniface VIII.

This extraordinary event was clothed with every form of legality. Celestine V set forth "the legitimate causes" that had determined him: humility, the desire for a more perfect life, his physical and mental inadequacies which made it impossible longer to assure the Church's government in such difficult circumstances. The cardinals approved his decision. In his first bull Boniface VIII justified his accession to the pontifical throne by recalling the proper juridical forms through which Celestine V's renunciation had just been accomplished; furthermore, he evoked the examples of renunciation furnished by tradition. Ecclesiastical authorities did not hesitate from then on to recognize him, and never were they forced to doubt that he was the legitimate pope.

Popular opinion was far from being as calm. Cleverly exploited by the Spirituals and the two Colonna cardinals, the moral prestige associated with Celestine V's person after his "Great Refusal" attracted every kind of sympathy to him. His goings and comings about Italy while he was endlessly fleeing to find deeper solitude; the miracles which, it was said, were the signs everywhere of his passing; the strict watch that Boniface VIII had imposed on him: these things made him a worker of miracles and a martyr in the eyes of the faithful. Boniface VIII feared a schism, and dread of this stayed with him until Celestine's death (May 19, 1296).

In France, from the beginning of 1295, Cardinal Simon de Beaulieu had expressed doubts about Boniface VIII's legitimacy. Playing up to the ill will of Philip the Fair for Boniface VIII, whose legate in France he had agreed to be, he launched this new argument into a turmoil of conflicting passions and interests. The Spirituals of southern France grieved for Celestine V, who had favored them. They too showed no hesitation about exploiting his renunciation in order to stir up discontent against Boniface VIII. But the legists of Philip the Fair and the Spirituals were going to run into an insuperable obstacle: the agreement of the theologians that the renunciation was justified.

The first theological writings we have on the renunciation are in a letter of the Franciscan master Pierre-Jean d'Olieu, dated September 14, 1295, at Narbonne. The Franciscan Conrad d'Offida was one of the Spirituals who had asked and obtained from Celestine V that he make them independent of the Order of Friars Minor: he had explained that he was not satisfied in seeing a pope to whom he owed so much remove himself from power. P. J. d'Olieu refuted on his account some of the objections raised against this renunciation. First he invoked an argument from fact: according to tradition a pope who falls into manifest heresy can be deposed; therefore pontifical power is not something incapable of being lost. A theological distinction confirmed this argument: the powers of order and of jurisdiction are separable, and if the pope can renounce the second without ceasing to possess the first, he can cease to be pope without ceasing to be a bishop. Obviously he had no superior to accept his renunciation; but then he did not have one to ratify his election either. It was objected that the marriage contracted by the Bishop of Rome with the Church Universal was indissoluble: P. J.

d'Olieu resolved this special argument by insisting on the differences between this spiritual marriage and the sacrament of marriage.

From the same year 1295 on, the question of the renunciation was posed at the University of Paris. The first evidence of the discussions to which it gave rise is Question IV of Godefroid de Fontaines' *Quodlibet* XII.[1] He invoked the arguments already presented by P. J. d'Olieu, while developing them further: they were only an adaptation for the case of the Sovereign Pontiff of traditional views on the renunciation of lesser prelates. But Godefroid de Fontaines added a new argument, one drawn from the [Aristotelian] principle of the final cause: the end of the sovereign pontificate being the utility of the Church, the pope who avows himself incapable of assuring it is not only authorized but obliged in conscience to renounce this charge. This involved no more than application of a general principle: no obligation freely accepted can bear prejudice against charity; just as a religious always keeps the right to place himself under a more rigorous rule if he judges this necessary for his salvation, so the pope can renounce a style of life that he judges prejudicial to the salvation of his soul.

In the following year, 1296, the question was taken up again at the University of Paris, by Pierre d'Auvergne. As we shall see, he made great progress toward achieving a solution. The argument based on final cause was confirmed by new authorities; the list of examples of renunciations was enriched and explained by an analogy borrowed from the Old Testament; the objections were

resolved with greater precision — such was the object of Question XV of Pierre d'Auvergne's first *Quodlibet*. . . .

Pierre d'Auvergne set forth his thesis in the form of a syllogism. What is permitted in theory by the Universal Church can be done in fact, for the Church authorizes nothing that it knows to be unjust; but the Universal Church permits renunciation, even as was evident in the case of Pope Celestine; therefore renunciation can take place legitimately. . . .

The fact that the pope has no superior to accept his renunciation in no way diminishes his right to it. Acceptance by the superior is required only in instances where a superior exists. Therefore the pope renounces on his own authority. If he does so after having taken counsel with the cardinals, he still renounces on his own responsibility, not theirs. Renunciation takes place in the presence of the cardinals, or of a general council, but not by virtue of their authority.

Thus did the pope's right to renounce his see find itself theoretically justified. This right was affirmed by Celestine V before his renunciation: it was therefor absolutely necessary to admit it. . . .

In 1297 P. J. d'Olieu again raised the problem of the renunciation. For him, as for Pierre d'Auvergne, the question was resolved in fact by Celestine's authentic declaration. As for doctrinal justification, he sought it first in the power possessed exclusively by the pope "himself to invalidate all doubts about the faith and to end all important controversies that could arise in the Church." After recalling at length the Scriptural and traditional foundations of this universal jurisdiction of the pope, P. J. d'Olieu applied them to the right possessed by the pope to renounce even his own power. The rest of his exposition

---

[1] A *quodlibet* is a characteristic form of scholastic disputation. — *Ed.*

only reproduced and developed the arguments he had presented in his letter of 1295.

In the same year, 1297, and with his usual prolixity, Giles of Rome composed his treatise *De renunciatione papae*. He . . . recalled again the separability of the power of order and the power of jurisdiction; he then presented a veritable treatise on the origin of power in general and in the Church, on the universal and monarchical character of the pope's power, and on the assistance that Divine Providence brings to the government of the Church. After this he enumerated the examples of renunciation already invoked by others . . . and justified them by philosophical arguments no longer based on only the final cause, but on all four [Aristotelian] causes. This treatise was both a justification for the conduct of Celestine V and an apology for Boniface VIII. The renunciation of the first had been invoked to place in doubt the legitimacy of the second and substitute for him a legitimate pope; Giles of Rome demonstrated that this argument was not convincing: never in the course of a rather long exposition does he consider any hypothesis for a legitimate pope other than that of voluntary renunciation. Only in the case of manifest heresy could the pope be deposed in spite of himself, but in that case he would have already ceased to be pope by the very act of losing his faith.

During the winter of 1302–1303 John of Paris devoted the last chapter of his treatise *De potestate regia et papali* to the question of renunciation. In the course of this work John of Paris reveals himself as a theologian who was profound, moderate, and original. These qualities seem to leave him, however, when he raises the question of the re-nunciation. He was content to borrow his case from two of the people who had preceded him, here and there adding a few suggestions suited to his own taste, which sufficed to orient the solution in a new way. He faithfully recapitulated Giles of Rome, whom he sometimes quoted exactly, and he inserted a few complementary arguments unscrupulously borrowed from Godefroid de Fontaines. But John of Paris's personal views helped to extend the doctrine of his predecessors dangerously, by applying to the pope's deposition the principles they had invoked to justify only his voluntary renunciation: since pontifical power was capable of being lost, since it was permitted the pope to renounce his charge if he judged himself incapable of filling it, was it not logical that he could be deposed in spite of himself, even in cases other than heresy, by those who watched over the Church's interests and regarded him as impotent to safeguard them? One senses the dangerous paths such suggestions could lead to. Imprecise and cautious as they may have been in John of Paris's treatise, they were a presentiment of the new policy of Philip the Fair.

The firmness with which the theologians — particulary John of Paris — had recognized the renunciation as legitimate forced Philip the Fair and his lawyers to rely upon other charges in their indictment of Boniface VIII. . . . Presented with the fact of the renunciation, five masters of theology of the University of Paris had successively recognized it as licit: Godefroid de Fontaines, Pierre d'Auvergne, P. J. d'Olieu, Giles of Rome, and John of Paris had shown themselves unanimous on this point in spite of the divergence of sympathies they bore toward the persons in conflict and in spite of their disagreements on many points of political theory.[2]

French policy had to change its methods; . . . the theme of illegitimacy owing to defective election gave place to the theme of illegitimacy because of heresy and other crimes. The attacks on Boniface VIII became the more pernicious once his own character was at stake, but at least the principles that justified the renunciation were safe.

---

[2] The range of their normal opinions was in fact enormous. Of the two best known, Giles of Rome was usually a strong supporter of papal authority, while John of Paris leaned toward acceptance of an independent royal power. —*Ed.*

Although Boniface VIII seemingly abandoned the positions that had led to his first clash with Philip the Fair, the Papal Jubilee of 1300 reanimated his spirits and led to a renewal of the quarrel. While historians have naturally differed on the emphasis to be placed on the various incidents associated with the Jubilee, they are in general agreement on their importance for ensuing events. In the following account, FÉLIX ROCQUAIN (1833–1925) presents an interpretation mildly suspicious of Boniface's actions and motives. At the same time, however, his treatment of Philip the Fair's response should be carefully analyzed because it suggests that the pope was not alone in his tendency to prefer questionable or extreme measures. Félix Rocquain wrote widely on the history of the medieval papacy, and is known also for his studies of eighteenth-century and Revolutionary France.*

Félix Rocquain

Two Hostile Sovereigns
at the Brink

Open opposition of princes to the Holy See's intervention in their temporal affairs, attacks getting ever more violent against the court of Rome, ideas of reform that were beginning to be precise and which attacked both the constitution of the papacy and that of the Church: such was the situation that an attentive observer could have noted when the famous Jubilee of 1300 opened at Rome. It is well known how Boniface in a solemn rescript had announced that full and complete remission of sins would be accorded to all those who would visit the tombs of the apostles during that year. He had, however, in a private bull excepted from these graces Frederick, king of Sicily, the subjects of Frederick's kingdom, the Colonnas, and, in a general manner, all enemies "present and future" of the Roman Church. Independent of the great number of ecclesiastics who came to Rome out of piety or to comply with the pope, the faithful responded to Boniface's appeal far beyond his expectation. Despite the violent criticisms being leveled against the court of Rome, even despite the unequivocal germs of a certain skepticism, during the course of the year nearly two hundred thousand foreigners, both ecclesiastic and secular, were counted at Rome, attracted not

*From Félix Rocquain, *La cour de Rome et l'esprit de réforme avant Luther* (Paris, Thorin & Fils, 1895), vol. 2, pp. 288–301. Reprinted by permission of Éditions E. de Boccard, Paris. Translated by Charles T. Wood. Some footnotes omitted.

only from the various regions of Italy, but from Spain, France, England, and Germany by the influence that religion continued to exercise on peoples everywhere, by curiosity about the Catholic splendors of Rome, and by the neverending fascination of the former city of the Caesars.

Historians are not agreed on the motives that led Boniface to institute the Jubilee. Some have maintained that he proposed by this means to attract Christianity's money to Rome. In fact the offerings of the faithful were so numerous that in the basilica of St. Paul priests were busy night and day gathering the money that fell at the foot of the apostle's altar. At the same time others have said, and more correctly, that Boniface, seeing faith growing weak, had hoped to reanimate it with this unusual spectacle of the Church's magnificence. Perhaps, too, he flattered himself with the thought that by enhancing the prestige of the Holy See he would thereby have more authority to impose peace on Europe and then to involve it in a crusade against the Infidels, a project he continued to support. . . . Another consideration could have been connected with these in the pontiff's mind. Boniface, who had just defeated the Colonnas, had learned, not without alarm, that they had escaped from the city where he had held them prisoner; he must have feared that they planned to recommence their hostile maneuvers, and he could have thought that he should dissipate the doubts they had spread about the legitimacy of his power by appearing to the eyes of the world in the full splendor of his dignity.

It is well known how, in the ceremonies of the Jubilee, Boniface showed himself to the faithful arrayed with the twin signs of spiritual and temporal authority and how he had the two swords borne before him, symbol of the two powers, while a herald at his side cried: "Here are the two swords; Peter, recognize your successor, and you, O Christ, behold your vicar." As congenial as this magnificance was to Boniface's ideas, in all likelihood there were special intrigues that led him to display his pontifical majesty in this manner. Right up to the opening of the Jubilee the Flemish ambassadors never stopped soliciting, in their master's name, the pope's protection against Philip the Fair, whose aggression the Count of Flanders at that point greatly feared. . . . [In early] January, 1300, . . . they remitted to Boniface a long note in which they, basing themselves intentionally on various texts from Scripture, said that the pope was the supreme judge, not only in spiritual things but in temporal things; that he held the place of Christ almighty and succeeded to all His rights in the empire of heaven and earth; that he could judge and depose the emperor, the first among the secular sovereigns, just as he could judge and depose the king of France, who pretended to have no superior to whose law he had to submit. It was in the private interests of the Count of Flanders to recognize in the head of the Church a political supremacy that princes were then agreeing to reject, but in fact this note was less the work of the Flemish deputies than of the cardinal of Acquasparta, one of the members of the Sacred College whose services they had purchased. On January 6, this cardinal, who enjoyed Boniface's particular confidence, developed in his turn the same doctrines in a sermon he preached in the presence of the pope and the other cardinals in the Lateran basilica. He demonstrated that "the pope alone has spiritual and temporal sovereignty over all men whoever they may be, in the place of God, by the gift that God made to St.

Peter," adding that "whosoever wishes to go against his will, the Church could go against, as against a miscreant, with the temporal and spiritual swords, by the authority and power of God." . . .

Whatever the reason for the institution of the Jubilee and the pope's resolution to show himself at it in ostentatious magnificence, the brilliant pomp of which this solemnity was the occasion, this extraordinary coming together of the faithful, who seemed to come from all parts of the earth, the partisan enticements of the cardinal of Acquasparta, and the adroit pleas of the Flemish deputies all converged to thrust Boniface into a state of exaltation toward which his own character already disposed him and which he was to retain until the end of his pontificate. He believed himself master of the world. In a constitution on canon law which he published this same year, he presented himself as the living law of the Church and declared that "the Roman pontiff bears all law in his breast." With regard to secular sovereigns, he no longer imagined that any could resist him. . . . As if he had been persuaded that it sufficed to give notice of his will to remove all obstacles and to vanquish all resistance, he said at the beginning of [one] letter: "The Roman pontiff, established by God above kings and kingdoms, is chief sovereign of the hierarchy in the Church Militant; seated on the throne of justice and placed by his dignity above all mortals, he pronounces his sentences with a tranquil soul and scatters all evils with his glance."

It was in this state of mind that Boniface attacked . . . a sovereign who was altogether the most powerful in Christendom and the most jealous of his independence: Philip the Fair. The quarrel began on the occasion of a legal action brought by the monarch against Bernard

Saisset, bishop of Pamiers. This prelate, accused of having wished to incite rebellion in Languedoc so that it would be taken from the crown of France and reunited with Aragon, had been arrested by the king's order, taken to his court, and placed as a prisoner under the guard of the archbishop of Narbonne. Such a trial violated the laws of the Church, according to which no bishop could be judged by secular courts.

Even before this affair was known in Rome, Boniface had many reasons for resenting Philip. He had seen, with dissatisfaction, how this prince had given asylum in his states to some of the fugitive Colonnas. . . . Moreover, he knew that Philip, abusing the concessions the Apostolic See had made him, was continuing to levy subsidies on the clergy without his kingdom's situation appearing to justify their necessity. Finally, Boniface never ceased to be roused against him by the Flemish deputies, who could now complain of the invasion of their country and the captivity of their sovereign. The affair of the bishop of Pamiers, coming in addition to these grievances, made Boniface's exasperation complete and he resolved to take severe action.

In the early days of December, 1301, many bulls were simultaneously dispatched to France. While in one Boniface summoned the king to place Bernard Saisset at liberty, he notified him in another that, going back on his previous concessions, he was depriving him of ecclesiastical subventions and suspending all the privileges granted up to that point by the Holy See to the crown of France.[1] To these letters was joined

---

[1] December 4, 1301 (bull *Salvator Mundi*). . . . In this bull he proclaimed these words which are another proof of that state of exaltation of which we have spoken: "The vicar of Christ can, agreeably

the famous bull *Ausculta fili* in which he reproached Philip not only for infringement of the Church's liberties and usurpation of the clergy's goods, but also for abuses in the administration of the kingdom, abuses carried to the point of debasing the coinage and oppressing his secular subjects. "Return," he said, "my dearest son, to the path that leads to God and from which you have strayed either through your own failing or at the instigation of evil counselors. Especially, do not let yourself be persuaded that you are without superior and that you are not under the head of the ecclesiastical hierarchy. Such an opinion is mad, and whoever holds it is an infidel cut off from the flock of the Good Shepherd." Boniface was not content to reproach the monarch severely for his conduct; he also announced to him that, in order to remedy the disorders of which this conduct was the cause, he had resolved to assemble a council at Rome on November 1 of the following year to which all the prelates of his kingdom would be summoned. "You can," he added, "come personally to this assembly or send deputies; we shall not hesitate to proceed, in your absence, however, should we judge it convenient." Finally, in a fourth bull Boniface informed the bishops of France of the meeting of the council and ordered them to come to it in order to make provision with him "for preservation of the Church's liberties, reformation of the kingdom, correction of the king, and good government in France."

This bull, *Ausculta fili,* in which Boniface made known his claim to be able to impose his will on the king as much

in matters that touched the temporal order as in those that pertained to the spiritual, had been drawn up in consistory and had been minutely studied before it was sent. This particularity proved that not only the pope but the cardinals too were unaware of the progress that opposition to the political supremacy of the Roman Church had made in men's minds since the death of Frederick II [1250], an opposition which had begun with the sovereigns and then won over the aristocracy and even people at large. When this bull became known in France, resistance was so lively and complete that opinion must nearly everywhere have been truly hostile to the pretensions of the Holy See.

Philip, who from the time of his battles with the king of England and the Count of Flanders had so openly refused to submit to the pontiff's authority, was still less disposed to submit to it in a situation where to him the independence of his crown must have appeared threatened. Up to now it has generally been believed, on the witness of certain chroniclers, that he had the bull *Ausculta fili* burned with great ceremony before the eyes of the people of Paris. Yet such an outburst was contrary to this prince's character. Jealous of his power and without scruple about the means that might be of service to defend or increase it, he did not like to commit himself, preferring to let his legists act or speak in his place, men who were both his counselors and his instruments; even in his boldest enterprises he preserved a seeming respect for law and religion. In place of *Ausculta fili* he substituted another shorter bull, one he made public and in which the pontiff's declarations were exaggerated and at the same time presented in the form most brutal and injurious to the king. After having tested

---

to the times, places, and persons, suspend, revoke, and modify statutes, privileges, and concessions that emanate from the Holy See without restriction of the plenitude of his authority by any other arrangement whatsoever."

public opinion with this fraud, he convoked to Paris the prelates and nobles of the kingdom along with the deputies of the towns so that they might, as he ordered them, "deliberate on certain affairs that in the highest degree interested the king, the kingdom, the churches, each and every one." This assembly, memorable for more reasons than one, took place on April 10, 1302, in the church of Notre Dame.

In this assembly, generally regarded as the first meeting in France of the Estates-General, one of Philip's legists, Pierre Flote, spoke in the king's name. He limited himself to interpreting the text of *Ausculta fili* (which he was careful not to read): "We have been sent," he said, "letters from the pope declaring that we must be submissive to him in the temporal government of our kingdom and that we hold the crown not of God alone, as people have always believed, but of the Apostolic See. Conformably with this declaration, the pontiff has called the prelates of this kingdom to a council at Rome to reform the abuses he says have been introduced by us and our officers in the administration of our Estates. You know, on the other hand, how the pope impoverishes the Church of France by conferring at his pleasure benefices whose revenues pass into foreign hands. You are not unaware how the churches are crushed by demands for tithes; how the metropolitans no longer have authority over their suffragans, nor the bishops over their clergy; how, in a word, the court of Rome, reducing the episcopate to nothing, draws all to it, power and money. These disorders must be stopped. We beg you, therefore, as master and friend to help us defend the liberties of the kingdom and those of the Church. As for us, we shall not hesitate, if it be necessary, to sacrifice for this double goal our goods, our life, and, if need be, those of our children."

Philip knew the temper of those to whom he spoke. By imputing to the pontiff the design of making the kingdom of France a fief of the court of Rome he succeeded without difficulty in stirring up the pride of the nobles, who proclaimed themselves ready on their part to maintain the independence of the crown at the price of their blood, and who drew up a collective letter in which they protested strongly against the pretensions of the Holy See. A similar letter was presented for the signature of the deputies from the towns. Both were sent, not to the pope, but to the cardinals, whom the king hoped, perhaps, to win to his interests by this seeming confidence.

As for the prelates—to whom Philip had made it clear that if they went to Rome he would regard them as his personal enemies—they addressed an embarrassed letter to Boniface in which, while straining to treat both parties with respect, they in reality decided for the king against the pope. They insidiously reproduced—and with all details—the complaints put forward by the monarch about exactions and other excesses of power by which the pontifical court oppressed the clergy of the kingdom. They proclaimed themselves inclined to go to Rome to take part in the council; they begged, however, that Boniface dispense them from the obligation lest their obedience to the Holy See's orders produce resentments in the king whose consequences could only be disastrous for the Church; and they ended with these words, which, better than anything else, testify as to their state of mind: "At present," they wrote, "a complete break is being prepared between the kingdom and the Church and, generally speaking, between the people and the clergy. Already laymen show only too clearly their aversion to us; not only do they scorn ecclesiastical censures, no matter from whence they come; they shun us; they put us out of their assemblies as though we were guilty of treason toward them. We therefore humbly appeal to your prudence. In withdrawing the injunction you transmitted to us, you would be acting for our safety and you would likewise be preserving a union between the Church and this kingdom, which seems on the point of breaking."

Philip was mistaken in hoping to rally some of the cardinals to his cause. Whether they feared Boniface's wrath, or whether the interests of the Roman court appeared to them in this matter to be inextricably bound with those of the pontiff, they showed themselves in their reply to the nobles of the kingdom to be in complete accord with him. On his side Boniface addressed a vehement letter to the bishops, reproaching them for their weakness and sending them formal refusal to accede to their request. In the meantime, an event took place which, by seeming to impair Philip's power, could only strengthen the pope in his resolutions.

The Flemings, on whom Philip had placed the harshest of yokes after he had made himself master of their land, finally rose in rebellion and wiped out a French army before Courtrai [July 11, 1302], a disaster that in fact was soon going to be redressed by the striking [French] victory of Mons-en-Pevèle [August 18, 1304]. A certain number of the prelates of the kingdom, themselves emboldened by this event, went to Rome for the council of November 1 despite Philip's prohibitions.[2] The king, by ordering their temporal goods seized, further irritated Boniface, who then decided on new measures against Philip. On November 18, at the same time that he declared in one bull that whoever prevented the faithful from repairing to the Holy See was thereby excommunicated, he published the bull *Unam Sanctam* addressed to all Christendom.

[2] Boniface had summoned seventy-eight French bishops; thirty-six actually attended. That so many obeyed the papal summons is largely explained by the extent to which men viewed Courtrai as a judgment of God on Philip's policies. This was particularly the case because the three men Boniface had specifically accused of being the cause of royal hostility—Pierre Flote, Robert of Artois, and the Count of St. Pol—were all slain on the field of battle.—*Ed.*

As a historian of the Church, PHILIP HUGHES should again be consulted, because his sympathy with the Church's mission helps him to place Boniface's Jubilee and the growing antagonism toward France in a context different from that of Rocquain. No longer is the pope the instigator of the renewed quarrel; rather, he becomes the aggrieved party whose actions are seen as nothing more than the justifiable response of a man anxious to preserve the integrity of his office and of its God-given functions.*

Philip Hughes

The Papacy Renews Its Strength

As the new year 1300 approached there was, to a very unusual degree, all that popular interest which greets the coming of a new century, the usual vague expectation of coming good fortune, but this time heightened—no doubt very largely through the recent revival and popularisation of the prophecies of Abbot Joachim.[1] The numbers of the pilgrims bound for Rome began to increase, and when they arrived they showed themselves clamorous for the expected, extraordinary, spiritual favours. Once every hundred years, some of them were saying, by a special act of the divine mercy,

not only were a contrite man's sins forgiven, but (upon appropriate penance done) the punishment his guilt deserved was also remitted. Boniface VIII does not, by any means, seem either to have created this spirit of expectation or to have exploited it at all in the service of his public policy.[2] Apparently he did

[1] Abbot Joachim of Fiore, one of the principal sources of inspiration of the Spiritual Franciscans. —Ed.

[2] No act of Boniface VIII lent itself so easily to the calumny and caricature of the bitterly anti-papal historians of the sixteenth century (and their successors) or to the amusement and cynicism of the Voltaireans past and present. Mann, *Lives of the Popes,* Vol. XVIII, pp. 172–83, deals faithfully with the legends. Digard's note, *op. cit.* II, 24, is useful: "Since Michelet's eloquent pages about the Jubilee of 1300, historians have excelled themselves in presenting it as a great triumph for the papacy that really turned the pope's brain, and drove him to process through the streets of Rome robed as the Roman

little more than fulfil what, spontaneously, Christian piety was expecting of the Roman See when, by the bull of February 22, 1300, he instituted the Holy Year of Jubilee. It is, in effect, a grant "to all who, being truly penitent, and confessing their sins, shall reverently visit these Basilicas [of St. Peter and St. Paul] in the present year 1300 . . . and in each succeeding hundredth year, not only a full and copious, but the most full pardon of all their sins."

The news of the great concession brought pilgrims to Rome by the hundred thousand, and from every part of Christendom, as a mass of contemporary literature testifies; and this novel and unmistakable evidence of what the papacy's spiritual power meant to the Christian millions seems greatly to have affected Boniface VIII.

To the pope too, it has been argued, the Jubilee was a year of special graces. The spring of this Jubilee year saw a joint embassy to Boniface from Philip the Fair and the new emperor Albert of Habsburg, and it saw also an anti-papal revolution at Florence: events that were the occasion, and the opportunity, for a reawakening in Boniface of his natural spirit of independence. But the enthusiasm of the hundreds of thousands of pilgrims did more than put new heart into the pope, a man now approaching his seventieth year. This concrete demonstration of universal faith in his supernatural office recalled to him in overwhelming force his first duty to be the father and shepherd of all Christian souls —so it is argued. The whole burden of

---

Emperor, as a legend we have dealt with elsewhere relates." Legends die hard and the Bampton Lectures for 1942 show this as still surviving; *cf.* Jalland, *The Church and the Papacy*, 417 *n.* Boase notes (p. 237) Boniface as being away from Rome during most of this Jubilee year.

Benedict Gaetani's case against Celestine V had been that the pope was too weak to defend the Church's freedom against the princes. But what else had Boniface VIII done, for years now, but surrender to princes?

At the audiences given now to the French ambassador, the pope made no secret of his suspicions of Flotte's designs. Tuscany, he declared, was the pope's by right. The very empire itself was the creation of the Holy See, "All the Empire's honour, pre-eminence, dignity, rights" being, as he wrote at this time to the Duke of Saxony, "derived from the liberality, the benevolence and gift of this see." As popes have set up, so they can tear down. Tuscany is a centre of discontent and hate, and so "for the honour of God, peace of Christendom, of the Church, of his vassals and subjects," the pope has determined to bring it once more under the rule of the Church. The authority of the apostolic see suffices for this. The Florentines were reminded of the same truths. The pope is the divinely appointed physician of all men's souls and sinners must accept his prescriptions. To hold any other theory is folly, for any other theory would mean that there are those in this world whom no law binds, whose crimes may go unpunished and unchecked.

Full of this new strength, Boniface brushed aside now the attempt of the French ambassadors to bully him with tales of what his enemies were saying about his private life and his faith, and taking up the complaints that came in from France about the attacks on the jurisdiction of the bishops, he sent to the king the letter *Recordare Rex Inclyte* (July 18, 1300). This is a remonstrance after the style of the letter—*Ineffabilis Amoris*—which had so roused the king in 1296. Boniface, as though that storm—and the defeat it brought— had never been, now told the king roundly that his usurpation of jurisdiction was seriously sinful, and that God would surely punish him for it did he not amend. The pope had, indeed, shown himself patient, but he could not be dumb for ever. In the end he must, in conscience, punish the king if the wrongdoing continued; and the tale of that wrongdoing is mounting up in the files. As for Philip's advisers, these are false prophets: it is from God's grace alone that his eternal salvation will come.

From the stand taken in this letter Boniface never retreated, though it was to bring him within an ace of violent death.

Philip was too busy with the last preparations for the conquest of Flanders to make any retort, but when Flotte went to Rome in the following November (1300), the atmosphere of the court was very different from what it had been at Orvieto three years earlier. "We hold both the swords," Boniface is reported as saying, and Flotte as replying, "Truly, Holy Father: but your swords are but a phrase, and ours a reality." But there was no break of relations, and the French sent Charles of Valois into Italy to help in the double task of subduing Florence and Sicily. What brought the break was Philip's arrest of the Bishop of Pamiers in the summer of 1301. Serious charges were of course made against the prelate; he was lodged in the common prison, then taken under guard to Paris to stand his trial before the king's court. But his innocence or guilt was a detail beside the real issue, the right of the king to try him, and the fact that the king could trample down with impunity the most sacred of all clerical rights in public law.[3] There is no doubt that this was a delib-

erately engineered *cause célèbre*, whose success would mark a new era for the expanding royal jurisdiction, and greatly discredit the ecclesiastical world before the nation.[4] And mixed up with the charges against the bishop there was a quarrel about the jurisdiction of the Inquisition, in which prominent Franciscan Spirituals attacked the Dominican inquisitors, and in which it was made very evident that in Languedoc the Albigensian movement was still a power under the surface of life. It is one of the several ways in which Philip the Fair recalls our own Henry VIII that now, while leading a life of blameless Catholic orthodoxy, he was secretly patronising and encouraging these heretics and rebels against the Church as an obvious move in the business of bringing pressure to bear on the pope.

---

[4] "It is the hand of Nogaret, and can be no other. It is a new system, a hideous perversion of law, by men of great skill as legalists, who know how to twist procedures and claim justice for them, and who understand only too well the passions and dark interests of their time, how to appeal to them, and make their excitement serve some ignoble purpose. It is the *cause célèbre* as a political force, lacking only means of publicity to rouse the unsavoury clamour of the mob, but hampered by no theories of admissible evidence, and broadening its effects to make them verbally transmissible and immediately striking. And under the protection of gloating public opinion, new abuses become possible, secret inquests, unwarned arrests, torture, overruling of resistance by sudden presentation of some horrid *fait accompli*. By these means fell the Templars; by these means was the posthumous trial of Boniface conducted; only more darkly, more daringly, more ingeniously, for this case of Pamiers is a first essay.... The spiritual powers will lie after this very much at the king's mercy." Boase, *Boniface VIII*, p. 300.

Dom Leclercq, also, notes how "the analogy between the methods employed in the trials of Boniface, of the Bishop of Pamiers, of the Templars and of Guichard de Troyes, reveals a single manoeuvring mind at work . . . [features that] give a family likeness to a set of trials which, actually, are very individual things. Another trait in which they are alike is that, in all cases, it is difficult to bring legal proof that the charges are false. The crimes faked in Nogaret's imagination are all crimes done in secret." H-L., VI, pt. i (1914), p. 578.

---

[3] The right of clerics to be tried only in Church courts.—*Ed.*

It was late October (1301) before the trial of the Bishop of Pamiers came on. It went well for the king until, in November, the Archbishop of Rheims made a strong, formal protest, in a Provincial Council, held at Compiègne, against the whole business of the bishop's arrest. The council, indeed, laid an interdict on all who, in contravention of the canon law, arrested a cleric. If a cleric so arrested should be transported to another diocese, the diocese in which he was arrested was "interdicted," and the domains of the authority responsible for the arrest. A certain amount of skilful juggling by the king's legists and the more subservient of the French bishops did indeed soon find a way through this law. But the moral effect of the declaration of Compiegne was very great, and nowhere was it more welcome than at Rome. It was indeed the first real check to the king from the French bishops for many years, the first unmistakable sign to the pope that there were bishops in France on whom he could rely.

But Boniface had not waited for this sign before taking the offensive. Flotte had written him a lying account of the trial, but it crossed a packet from the pope with a whole batch of strong, decisive letters for France. The revelations in the Pamiers case that the king was backing the Spirituals and the Albigenses, attacking the Inquisition, and that the mass of the French bishops were looking on indifferently at a most spectacular attack on the rights of their order, lifted the pope above the mere diplomatic game. From now on his action has the grave, apostolic quality of Hildebrand himself.

In these letters, written in the first week of December 1301, the pope demands that the Bishop of Pamiers be set free and allowed freely to make his way to Rome. He suspends all those privileges granted to Philip in the matter of clerical taxation and church property. He summons all the bishops of France to a council, to be held in Rome (in November 1302) where the whole question of the state of religion in France, and of the king's government of the country, will be examined; to this council the king is also invited, either to come in person or be represented there. Finally there is a letter, a confidential letter, for the king. This is the bull *Ausculta Fili,* 5 December, 1301, which as handled by the French, played a most important part in the events of the next eighteen months.

In many ways this letter hardly differs from the remonstrances which Boniface had already sent to the king. It tells him that his sins, as a Catholic ruler oppressing the rights of the Church, are notorious and a bad example to all Christendom. It lists these acts of usurpation and adds the crime of debasing the coinage. It again warns the king against his advisers, and points out that the whole of France is restive under their harsh, oppressive rule. The king cannot make the ministers an excuse for his sins: and the pope urges him to take part in the coming council. If he does not appear, its business will go forward without him. But all this somewhat familiar lecture acquires a new gravity from the opening passage of the letter, in which there is an extremely clear statement of the king's subject-status in relation to the pope, a statement in which we may read yet a further contribution to the controversy now engaged in which Dante, Pierre Dubois and the two great Augustinian theologians, Giles of Rome and James of Viterbo, are playing leading parts.[5] The Church has but

_____

[5] Dante and Dubois (a French publicist) maintained the independence of secular power while Giles of Rome and James of Viterbo insisted on the all-inclusive authority of the spiritual power and of the pope.—*Ed.*

a single head, Boniface reminds the king, and this head is divinely appointed as a shepherd for the whole flock of Christ. To suggest, then, that the King of France has no earthly superior, that he is not in any way subject to the pope is madness, is indeed, the prelude to infidelity. This doctrinal note is to appear again, and still more strikingly, in the controversy.

Ausculta Fili was not a manifesto nor a public state paper, but a confidential letter sent privately to the king: and therein lay Flotte's opportunity. The bull was no sooner read than destroyed, and a tendentious summary of it drawn up, to be the basis of a most effective, national, anti-papal compaign. This summary—called *Deum Time* from its opening words—Flotte first submitted to a conference of theologians and legists. It adapted the teaching and claims of the first part of Boniface's letter to cover power and jurisdiction in the temporal sphere. The pope is now skilfully made to appear as claiming to be, because pope, the king's feudal overlord; the pope's consent is needed, then, for the validity of all such acts as subinfeudation, and all the grants made so far for centuries must be invalid; also the king, as vassal to the pope, is liable for aids to the pope in all his wars.

This preparatory work done, it now remained to ask the nation's opinion on the papal claim as thus stated. The setting for this was the famous church of Notre Dame in the capital where, on April 10, 1302, representatives of the clergy, the nobles and the towns came together in the presence of the king. Flotte made a great speech, in the king's name, expounding the thesis of *Deum Time,* adding that the pope's citing the king to appear before him at Rome was a sample of what all had now to expect, the crown of all those usurpations of the Church of Rome on the Church of France under which, for years now, true religion had been withering away. The King of France had no superior as a temporal ruler; he stood out as the real champion of religion. And Flotte ended with an appeal to the nation to support Philip.

In the debate which followed, the suggestion was made that Boniface was a heretic and the nobles set their seals to a letter which, ignoring the pope, recounted to the college of cardinals all the charges made against Boniface, to whom they only referred as "he who at the moment occupies the seat of government in the church"; and, an incendiary statement surely, they say that "never were such things thought of except in connection with antiChrist." Unanimously the laity pledged their support to the king.

The clergy were not so ready. They first asked for time to think it all over. It was refused them; they were told that opposition would only prove them the king's enemies. So they promised obedience to the king as vassals and asked leave to obey the pope, as they were bound, and to go to the Roman council. This also was refused them. And then they wrote to the pope, an anxious letter telling him that never had there been such a storm in France, never had the Church been in such danger, and begging the pope to abandon the plan for a council.

It was not until ten weeks later (24 June, 1302) that the delegates from the national assembly reached the pope with these letters. They were received in full consistory at Anagni, and two addresses were made to them, one by the Cardinal Matthew of Acquasparta and the other by the pope himself. The cardinal explained that the *Ausculta Fili* was the outcome of many weeks' deliberation between the pope and the cardinals, and he denied absolutely the interpretation put upon it in France. It was a purely pastoral act of the pope who makes no claim in it to be the king's superior judge in temporal matters but who, all men must allow, is the judge whether those whose office it is to exercise temporal power do so in accordance with morality or not.

The pope spoke most vigorously. He reprobated the chicanery which, evidently, had falsified for the public his message to Philip. He denounced Flotte by name as the real author of the mischief and with him Robert of Artois and the Count of St. Pol; they would, he prophesied, come to a bad end. Once again he gave warning that the French were hated everywhere; all Europe would rejoice when the hour of their defeat arrived. The king seemed not to realise it, but the facts were that he was on the brink of disaster. As for the council—this to the clergy—it must take place and, severely rebuking the cowardice of the bishops, the pope threatened the defaulters with deposition from their sees.

The cardinals sent a written reply to the letter from the nobles and in it they severely reproved their neglect to give the pope his proper style, and their reference to him by "an unwonted and insolent circumlocution."

Drama was never lacking at any stage of this long-drawn-out controversy, but now it touched the heights. While all France was being rallied to the support of the king against the pope, the French invasion of Flanders had begun. Philip had now to meet, however, not merely the feudal levies of his rebellious vassal the Count, but the enraged craftsmen of the towns. And before the envoys to Boniface had returned with the news of the pope's lurid warnings, barely a fortnight after the scene in the consistory, the French army suffered one of the greatest defeats of its history, outside the walls of Courtrai, at the hands of Peter de Koninck and his weavers (Battle of the Golden Spurs, 11 July, 1302). And among those slain were the three men whom the pope had singled out by name, Flotte, Robert of Artois, and the Count of St. Pol.

Philip the Fair was now in full retreat, and not alone from Flanders, now lost to the French crown for ever. He no longer sounded defiance to the pope, but allowed the bishops to explain, apologetically, that they could not leave their sees at such a national crisis; and he sent an embassy to represent him at the council, an embassy which made full recognition of Boniface as pope (October 7, 1302).

Of what passed at the council we have no knowledge, but nearly half of the French bishops took part in it (39 out of 79). The pope had so far softened towards the beaten king that there was no repetition of the events at Lyons, sixty years before, when a council had tried and deposed the emperor Frederick II. There was no trial of Philip the Fair in 1303, nor sentence or declaration against him. The solitary outcome of the proceedings was a general declaration to the whole Church, the most famous act of Boniface's career, the bull *Unam Sanctam* (November 18, 1302).

Unam Sanctam is unquestionably the most famous bull issued by BONIFACE VIII, if not by any pope. Its language is both stately and lucid, but the clarity with which it is seemingly written has tended to disappear under scholarly scrutiny. Wide differences of opinion have been voiced over Boniface's intentions in the document, and even those who agree on its meaning have had violent differences over the reasons for its hostile reception in France. In analyzing this bull, therefore, the reader should be sensitive both to Boniface's probable purpose and to Philip's likely reaction.*

Boniface VIII

Unam Sanctam

That there is one holy, Catholic and apostolic church we are bound to believe and to hold, our faith urging us, and this we do firmly believe and simply confess; and that outside this church there is no salvation or remission of sins, as her spouse proclaims in the Canticles, "One is my dove, my perfect one. She is the only one of her mother, the chosen of her that bore her" (Canticles 6:8); which represents one mystical body whose head is Christ, while the head of Christ is God. In this church there is one Lord, one faith, one baptism. At the time of the Flood there was one ark, symbolizing the one church. It was finished in one cubit and had one helmsman and captain, namely Noah, and we read that all things on earth outside of it were destroyed. This church we venerate and this alone, the Lord saying through his prophet, "Deliver, O God, my soul from the sword, my only one from the power of the dog" (Psalm 21:21). He prayed for the soul, that is himself, the head, and at the same time for the body, which he called the one church on account of the promised unity of faith, sacraments and charity of the church. This is that seamless garment of the Lord which was not cut but fell by lot. Therefore there is one body and one head of this one and only church, not two heads as though it were a monster, namely Christ and Christ's vicar, Peter and Peter's successor, for the Lord said to this Peter, "Feed my sheep" (John 21:17). He said

*Brian Tierney, *The Crisis of Church & State 1050–1300,* © 1964. Reprinted by permission of Prentice-Hall, Inc., Englewood Cliffs, New Jersey. Pp. 188–189.

"My sheep" in general, not these or those, whence he is understood to have committed them all to Peter. Hence, if the Greeks or any others say that they were not committed to Peter and his successors, they necessarily admit that they are not of Christ's flock, for the Lord says in John that there is one sheepfold and one shepherd.

We are taught by the words of the Gospel that in this church and in her power there are two swords, a spiritual one and a temporal one. For when the apostles said "Here are two swords" (Luke 22:38), meaning in the church since it was the apostles who spoke, the Lord did not reply that it was too many but enough. Certainly anyone who denies that the temporal sword is in the power of Peter has not paid heed to the words of the Lord when he said, "Put up thy sword into its sheath" (Matthew 26:52). Both then are in the power of the church, the material sword and the spiritual. But the one is exercised for the church, the other by the church, the one by the hand of the priest, the other by the hand of kings and soldiers, though at the will and suffrance of the priest. One sword ought to be under the other and the temporal authority subject to the spiritual power. For, while the apostle says, "There is no power but from God and those that are ordained of God" (Romans 13:1), they would not be ordained unless one sword was under the other and, being inferior, was led by the other to the highest things. For, according to the blessed Dionysius, it is the law of divinity for the lowest to be led to the highest through intermediaries. In the order of the universe all things are not kept in order in the same fashion and immediately but the lowest are ordered by the intermediate and inferiors by superiors. But that the spiritual power

excels any earthly one in dignity and nobility we ought the more openly to confess in proportion as spiritual things excel temporal ones. Moreover we clearly perceive this from the giving of tithes, from benediction and sanctification, from the acceptance of this power and from the very government of things. For, the truth bearing witness, the spiritual power has to institute the earthly power and to judge it if it has not been good. So is verified the prophecy of Jeremias [1.10] concerning the church and the power of the church, "Lo, I have set thee this day over the nations and over kingdoms" etc.

Therefore, if the earthly power errs, it shall be judged by the spiritual power, if a lesser spiritual power errs it shall be judged by its superior, but if the supreme spiritual power errs it can be judged only by God not by man, as the apostle witnesses, "The spiritual man judgeth all things and he himself is judged of no man" (1 Corinthians 2:15). Although this authority was given to a man and is exercised by a man it is not human but rather divine, being given to Peter at God's mouth, and confirmed to him and to his successors in him, the rock whom the Lord acknowledged when he said to Peter himself "Whatsoever thou shalt bind" etc. (Matthew 16:19). Whoever therefore resists this power so ordained by God resists the ordinance of God unless, like the Manicheans, he imagines that there are two beginnings, which we judge to be false and heretical, as Moses witnesses, for not "in the beginnings" but "in the beginning" God created heaven and earth (Genesis 1:1). Therefore we declare, state, define and pronounce that it is altogether necessary to salvation for every human creature to be subject to the Roman Pontiff.

T. S. R. Boase

The Pope's Political Dynamite

Unscrupulous and shifty, in face of
the disaster in Flanders Philip remained
admirably resolute. The reply to the
letters from Rome was a renewal of the
prohibition of export and an order that
no clerics should leave the country. When
England at once sent new envoys, hoping
for terms from the disabled king, Philip
declared that he would no longer accept
Benedict Caetani's mediation, and that,
if the King of England wished to discuss
terms, he must come in person. It was a
bold front. But it could not hide his in-
security. In person—and rarely is Philip's
personal action so evident as after this
sudden loss of Flotte—he led an army into
Flanders, but it accomplished nothing.

The towns held firm, the Flemings remained on the defensive. Philip did not
dare to risk another crushing defeat.
Short of supplies, baulked, nothing accomplished he had to beat a retreat in
October.

The country did not share its ruler's
confidence. The Duke of Burgundy,
whom Boniface had suggested as a mediator, was in correspondence with several
cardinals, in particular with Matthew
Rosso, who wrote warning the duke that
Philip had incurred excommunication.
Matthew's letter had none of Boniface's
vague terms of empire, but it was very
definite as to the inalienable privileges
of the church. . . . Many of the French

---

*From T. S. R. Boase, *Boniface VIII* (London: Constable & Company Ltd., 1933), pp. 315–323. Footnotes
omitted.

clergy, disregarding the royal prohibition, journeyed to Rome for the council.

On 30 October it opened. Of the seventy-eight bishops of France whom the pope had summoned, thirty-six were present. But of these Peter Mornay of Auxerre was on an embassy for the king, the Bishop of Chalons was on business connected with his election and was a royal sympathiser, and the Bishops of Noyon, Coutances and Béziers had brought the appeal of the clergy and were all three supporters of Philip. Of the remaining thirty-one, the greater part came from the Archbishoprics of Bordeaux, Auch, and Bourges: Tours was partially represented, as was Narbonne, and the French bishoprics of Lyons: apart from Brittany the north was completely absent. Of the four archbishops attending, Giles of Bourges had long been resident in Rome and was a well-known papal propagandist; Bordeaux was Bertrand of Got, the future Clement V, a man of conciliatory temper, whose post had peculiar difficulties in relation to the dispute over Guienne. He had opposed Philip on various points of suzerainty, but had not apparently gained his ill-will; his diocese could clearly not be judged by the same standard of obsequiousness as was expected elsewhere. Reginald of Montbason, Archbishop of Tours, a pre-Bonifascian appointment, had on the whole little cause to feel well disposed to Rome . . . but Reginald was anxious to keep in with all parties, and came to Rome as readily as in the following summer he attended at the Louvre to sign Philip's anti-papal proclamation. The Archbishop of Auch was a staunch papal adherent, and carried his bishops with him. Throughout the struggle, Paris, where so many of the king's prominent ministers were southerners, completely failed to influence the south.

This local and limited support was hardly sufficient for any great papal demonstration. It was possible to excuse some absentees on grounds of health or age: Rouen was playing little part in public concerns: Walter of Bruges at Poitiers could hardly be considered a royalist and the Bishop of Arras was an Anagniote of known loyalty: but they remained excuses. The French church was manifestly divided in its adherence, and the presence of six important abbots (but not including him of St. Denis)[1] was little compensation where the issues were so largely concerned with the administration of the secular church. It was, moreover, a galling thought that the strength of the opposition lay in recent appointments, and that papal compliance with royal wishes was now meeting an ungenerous return.

The acts of the council were later destroyed, but they were not numerous. "There was much talk but not much done," one chronicler said of it. Flotte's memory was condemned, and his sons and relatives deprived of all their ecclesiastical dignities: Philip was not formally attacked: some of the French clergy were doubtless a moderating influence, averse to all extreme measures. It is probable that the council was no longer sitting, when on 18 November a bull was drawn up excommunicating all who prevented the faithful from coming to Rome. But the proximity of date lent this decision some conciliar authority, as happened also in the case of a far more famous document, drawn up on the same day, the bull *Unam Sanctam*. . . .

---

[1] St. Denis was the royal abbey just outside of Paris where the kings of France were buried.—*Ed.*

Amongst Boniface's bulls it has a distinctive position. It is for him curiously impersonal, though an early tradition has ascribed it completely to his composition. The whole form and wording of it is as of a general statement detached from any particular circumstances: even the French are nowhere specifically mentioned, and the opponents of the power of the Holy See are merely described as "The Greeks and others who pretend that they are not subject to Peter and his successors." As has repeatedly been pointed out, it contains little new. It is a careful statement of the claims of the papacy to final sovereignty, and bases the claim on the divine origin of that power, not on any practical necessities, nor even historical precedents, for there is no mention of the transference of the empire or the deposition of the last Merovingian. It is as an "order established by God" that it must be obeyed: it is a power formally revealed by Christ to St. Peter, and as such it is an article of faith, necessary for salvation. This is the primary case for the papal power; it had often been stated before and the bull's greatest novelty is its absence of involved proof. Amid the controversial literature of the period it sounds a note of solemn and eloquent certainty.

Of the views of theorists of the time Boniface in fact avails himself little: he borrows phrases from them; it is clear that some at least he has read; but he does not incorporate their conclusions. Yet they are there, a background to the bull, and a background more visible to contemporaries than it is to us to-day. Of them, in ability and service, Giles of Rome, Archbishop of Bourges, former tutor of the King of France, defender of Boniface's legitimacy, was the most important. His *De ecclesiastica potestate* was probably written early in 1302: it was

known to Boniface before he drew up the bull, and it was equally known to Cardinal John the Monk, who wrote a commentary on *Unam Sanctam* in the winter of 1302–3. Giles puts forward the extreme view of papal supremacy. He has a very clear perception of the central problem: that there must be a hierarchy of powers, that one must be lesser than the other—if the temporal sword were not under the spiritual there would be no true order. It is through the church that all power is instituted, and it is only thus that dominion can be justly exercised, for it is through the church that it is spiritually regenerated and sacramentally absolved: through such grants alone can any lordship or even any proprietary rights be justly exercised.

These were far more extreme deductions than anything that Boniface expressed. In *Unam Sanctam* we find only a solemn statement, on the grounds of revealed faith, of the supremacy of the spiritual power, and it would be quite possible to accept a comparatively moderate view of the manner in which that supremacy was to be exercised. But Giles was his trusted adviser, singled out as such by the French court, and Boniface had in his mind, if not actually before his eyes, the book which the Archbishop of Bourges had lately "laid at his feet," and echoes memories of it in the words he chose. And in the papal circle were others, holding opinions as extreme, and being openly rewarded for expressing them.

To the same order as Giles, the Augustinian Hermits, belonged Augustinus Triumphus, and James Capocci of Viterbo. The former was an intimate friend and adviser of Charles of Naples, and played a considerable part as a pamphleteer in repelling the accusations brought against Boniface after his death, extolling the highest view of papal authority, of the spiritual as the ultimate *causa et principium* of corporal things. There is no writing of his that can certainly be assigned to a date as early as 1302, though he was an older man than either Giles or James of Viterbo, but his views must have been well known at Rome and Naples, and his reputation was one that carried weight. James of Viterbo, on the other hand, definitely produced his treatise *De regimine christiano* as a contribution to the disputes of 1302. It was dedicated to the pope "qui ad libertatem ecclesiastici regiminis et exaltationem Catholice veritatis prudenter et fragranter invigilat,"[2] and as its reward James was in September of that year created Archbishop of Benevento, only to be translated after three months to Naples at the special request of Charles II. His book is in many ways a modification of that of Giles, which had clearly preceded it. He cannot accept the latter's theory that the temporal power, unless regenerate through spiritual institution, is illegitimate and unjust: to him there is a *via media;* temporal authority comes from "the natural inclination of man," and therefore indirectly from God. But all human power is imperfect and unformed, unless formed and perfected through the spiritual. The temporal power is only complete and full when derived also from the spiritual power. Henry of Cremona, also, wrote his book *De potestate papae* expressly to rebut the murmurings against Pope Boniface: and, under the patronage of Richard of Siena (Henry himself had probably been employed on the Sext)[3] was nominated

Bishop of Reggio "on account of his writings" in spring of 1302, at a time when he was actually absent in France, on the celebrated embassy under James *de Normannis.* It is a straightforward tract, embodying most of the accepted scriptural proofs; the body is under the soul, the pope has authority over all souls, therefore all bodies are under the pope. A less original work than the others, it shows none of their insight into the problem as a political dilemma: but it is a competent piece of legal argument, backed by all the accepted precedents, and as such probably carried some weight in its day.

Such were the surroundings of the bull: and in France, hesitating on the edge of the final struggle, its clauses must have been read in the light of such commentary. "There is one holy Catholic and apostolic church that we are bound to recognise. Outside of it there is neither salvation nor pardon for sins." So the bull opens. Then follow symbols of this unity drawn by allegory from texts of the bible, "My dove, my undefiled is but one"; a quotation that Arnald of Villanova had used in his book, *De cymbalis ecclesiae,* to rebuke all discussions in synods or universities as to the supremacy of the pope. The unity of the church must be enforced within, before there is question of its relations without, with the temporal power.

"My dove is one" and "there is but one ark of Noah." "The church has only one head, not two as a monster." "When Christ said to Peter 'Feed my sheep,' he gave to him all, not some only. When the Greeks and others claim not to be subject to Peter and his successors, by that same claim they affirm that they are not members of the flock of Christ. For there shall be one fold and one shepherd." Then follows a passage on the two swords,

---

[2] "who prudently and agreeably watches over the liberty of ecclesiastical rule and the exaltation of Catholic truth." — *Ed.*

[3] The Sext was an addition to the corpus of Canon Law compiled on Boniface's order. — *Ed.*

closely following St. Bernard's exposition, the *locus classicus,* if not the earliest rendering of that analogy.

The remaining clauses are very closely based upon Giles: his theory of the need of order, that for one to be supreme another must be lower, is outlined: the greater dignity of the spiritual is affirmed by its receipt of tithe, by its anointing of kings, by its acceptance of power and by its exercise of government. It belongs to the spiritual power to institute the temporal and to judge it if its works are not good. Thus is fulfilled in the power of the church, the prophecy of Jeremiah. "See, I have this day set thee over the nations, and over the kingdoms." To institute *(instituere)* is capable of various meanings, and the sense of the bull has been at different times twisted accordingly to suit different cases, but the sense in the fourth chapter of Giles' *De potestate,* of which this passage is a close compression, is beyond question: the temporal power is brought into being through the spiritual. "For he that is spiritual judgeth all things, yet he himself is judged of no man." Power is by virtue of goodness, that which has most the true aim must most be able to direct: and, though the pope as man may not be the best man, his status is that of the best man, and he is enabled by the especial grant of divine grace made to Peter and his successors. "Though a man has received and exercised this power, yet it is not a human power, but divine. He who resists this power, resists the order established by God, or, like the Manichaeans, he believes in two principals, which is heresy. "Porro subesse romano pontifici, omni humanae creaturae declaramus, dicimus et diffinimus omnino esse, de necessitate salutis."[4] It is on the

divine charge to Peter that finally the papal power rests. It is matter of revelation and of faith. And now, in the midst of so much theorising and criticism, men are reminded of the fundamental basis of that which they are questioning. To this point had Boniface arrived: the supreme spiritual power can be judged by no man, but by God alone: his acts are under divine direction and based on a divine charge: no earthly power can claim an existence independent of him, and inasmuch as every act has a moral implication, it is submitted to his judgment. "Si deviat terrena potestas, iudicatur a potestate spirituali."[5] It is the claim of *Ausculta Fili* and of the speech in consistory; and there is nothing in the bull to contradict Boniface's earlier recognition of the right of the state to conduct its own business, to draw up right regulations. The Gelasian position must be maintained: *spiritualia* can be differentiated from *temporalia:* and there will be no intervention in *temporalia* as long as the moral law is not broken. But of that latter the papacy is the sole interpreter, judge and codifier, and to question this is to deny divine revelation. The creature may have some will and rights of its own, but it cannot question the creator, In no earlier statement had Boniface stressed the view that all temporal power must come through and from the spiritual. Marshalling his arguments, forestalling new lines of attack, he drew aside the veil from before the full splendour of the Holy See, and exposed its inner mystery to a world that now could only worship or rebel. There was to be no more accommodating doctrine: the light was now too strong for any patchwork of compromise to pass unnoticed.

---

[4] "Whence we declare, say and define that it is altogether necessary for salvation that all human creatures be subject to the Roman pontiff."—*Ed.*

[5] "If the earthly power errs, it may be judged by the spiritual power."—*Ed.*

Frequently a document's intended meaning is misconstrued by those reading it. Such was the case, argues JEAN RIVIÈRE (1878–1946), with *Unam Sanctam*. In what amounts to a line by line analysis of its provisions Rivière attempts to show that the pope's ideas were largely traditional and not very startling. If accepted, this view would greatly modify one's understanding of Boniface's motives and ambitions. Rivière was a French abbé and professor at the University of Strasbourg, best known for his work on medieval and patristic theology.*

Jean Rivière

Boniface's Theological Conservatism

The structure of the bull [*Unam Sanctam*] is far from simple. As in every text of this kind, the doctrinal definition that is set forth comes at the end of an argument designed to legitimize it by reconciling it with premises elsewhere regarded as certain. . . . One must distinguish between the propositions themselves and the arguments invoked to support them. These various materials are of unequal value, although all contribute to some extent to making us understand the extent of the pontifical constitution and the spirit of its author. The theologian adopts, in his field, the prudent attitude of the jurist, who takes great pains to indicate the difference between the purview of the law and the reasons behind its introduc-

tion, between the sentence of the court and the considerations that tend to justify it, all the while utilizing these related facts to explain the document brought for his interpretation.

It is evident above all that Boniface VIII wanted to place the rights of the Roman pontiff before the Catholic conscience. The final formula, where the last word of his thought is expressed, refers to the conditions necessary for salvation, affirming that submission to the pope enters in as an essential qualification: "It is entirely necessary for salvation . . . to be subject to the Roman Pontiff." The supernatural order has been determined by Christ and no one then contested that it had been concentrated

*From Jean Rivière, *Le Problème de l'église et de l'état au temps de Philippe le Bel* (Paris and Louvain: La Librairie Ancienne Honoré Champion, 1926), pp. 79–87. Reprinted by permission of Librairie H. Champion, Paris. Translated by Charles T. Wood. Footnotes omitted.

in the Church. As a result, it became a question of placing the role of the pope in this scheme of things in relief. Underlying the bull *Unam Sanctam*, therefore, is a theology of the Church and its mission which constitutes the doctrinal framework within which the function of the Sovereign Pontiff, its head, is inserted. The whole is related to the divine plan by means of the various resources that exegesis and philosophy offered to the minds of the time.

Although the development of this complex thesis does not always seem to follow a strictly rectilinear path, one can distinguish two related parts, one following the other: one poses the principles from which the other draws the consequences; the first sets forth the constitution of the Church, the second describes the powers that flow from it. These two themes will serve us as a key.

According to the formula of the old symbols, the Church is one, holy, Catholic, and apostolic; this is a dogma imposed on the Christian: "We are forced by faith firmly to believe." In proclaiming this in his turn, Boniface VIII insists on the unity and the uniqueness of this institution. The significant inversion with which the bull opens invites the translation: "There is only one Church," UNAM *sanctam Ecclesiam . . . credere cogimur . . . nosque hanc firmiter credimus et simpliciter confitemur* ["We are forced to believe in . . . one holy Church . . . and we firmly believe and sincerely confess this"]. That is why this first article of faith is soon joined by a second, which completes it: outside the Church there is neither grace nor salvation, "outside of which there is neither salvation nor remission of sins." In effect, the Church forms a sort of organism of which Christ is the head and which, as a result, is in a continuum with

God: "it represents one mystical body, whose corporal head is Christ, indeed the Godhead of Christ." Whence one can foresee that this organic unity must normally be translated outward by the unity of its head.

In accordance with the eclectic manner of the period, this doctrine is founded on the lyrical outpourings with which the bridegroom of the Song of Songs salutes his beloved and on the affirmations of Saint Paul, who declared that he recognized only one faith and one baptism as well as only one Lord. It is especially illuminated and clarified by the allegory of the ark, which has the advantage of uniting in one expressive image all the themes already indicated: unity of the Church and of its head, "one . . . ark of Noah prefiguring the one Church, which, completed in one cubit, had one ruler and helmsman"; absolute necessity of being a part of it to be saved: "outside of which, we read, all things . . . were destroyed." In the same sense the pope again brings up the passage where the Psalmist speaks of his "uniqueness" and of the "seamless garment" for which the tormentors of Christ cast lots to keep it from being cut—texts that serve him well in accentuating the intimate union between the Lord and His Church.

From these premises he immediately draws the alluring conclusion: the Church, being only of one body, must also, on pain of being a monster, have but one head. This unique "head" is obviously Christ. But Christ is continued in the person of his vicar: Boniface therefore returns to Peter, and to his successors, to strengthen him in his role as chief. All these deductions are mustered in a single sentence whose astonishingly full terms doubtless represent the maximum doctrinal density one could ever expect in the human language:

Therefore in this one and only Church there is one body, one head, not two heads like a monster: to wit, Christ and the vicar of Christ, Peter and Peter's successors.

In effect, it is to Peter that the risen Saviour has confided his sheep, not these particular sheep or those, but all without exception. The sheepfold of Christ is unique and so is the shepherd. Whoever attempts to flee from Peter like the schismatic Greeks, "either Greeks or others," would thereby renounce their right to be counted among the sheep of Christ: "they necessarily confess that they are not of Christ's sheep." The identification of the mystical with the social body follows logically from that of the invisible Christ with his representative. Association, fusion of the divine order with the human order, instruct us about both the role of the Church in the plan of salvation and the basic principles of its organization.

"The nature of the work follows from the nature of the being," say the schools: the powers of the Church conform to this view. Boniface VIII devotes the last part of the bull to expatiating on them, so the preceding generalities were doubtless intended as preparation.

At the outset the pope claims for the Church a double domain, spiritual and temporal. He expresses himself in the metaphor of the two swords, following current terminology: "In this [Church] and in its power are two swords, namely the spiritual and the temporal"—a doctrine that he believed could be read, with the aid of contemporary allegorizing theology, in the Gospels themselves. When the Apostles showed the Master the two swords they had to defend themselves, the latter did not say, "That is too much," but, "That is enough." Furthermore, to reply, as He did elsewhere, to Peter who had drawn his sword, "Put up *thy* sword in its sheath," was this not

to give proof that the "temporal sword" was in his power as well as the spiritual?

This demonstration is followed by an explanation that clarifies the point. There is this difference between the two swords: one is used by the Church, the other for the Church; that is, the temporal authority is in the hands of the prince, but always at the service of ecclesiastical authority and under its exalted direction:

Therefore both the spiritual and the temporal swords are in the power of the Church; but the latter must be used *for the Church* and the former *by the Church;* the former by the priest, the latter by the hand of kings and knights, but at the will and sufferance of the priest.

By their very nature, one sees that the powers of the temporal sovereign can only be subordinate. Boniface expressly underlines this aspect, so important for mutual relations:

The one sword, however, must be under the other and the temporal authority subjected to the spiritual power.

All this subsumes a kind of syllogism whose two propositions are successively justified. The subordination of powers refers to Providence's law of order, such as it was set forth by the blessed Dennis.[1] One cannot truly imagine that the works of God are not ordained, and the normal order is established by the hierarchical superposition: "divine law is led back from the lowest level via the middle ones to the highest." This being the case, it is clear that the spiritual power surpasses the temporal in nobility and worth, just as spirit surpasses matter. A rational pre-eminence, furthermore, can be seen inscribed on the significant features of

---

[1] Pseudo-Dionysius, an early sixth-century Christian writer with strong mystical and Neoplatonic overtones. — *Ed.*

historical reality: witness especially the custom of tithes, the anointing of sovereigns, and the control exercised by the Church over the failings of their government:

We see this clearly in the giving of tithes, both in blessing and sanctification, in the reception of that power, and in the governance of things. For, as truth testifies, the spiritual power has to institute and judge the earthly power, if it be not good.

Although he is only thinking of Scriptural texts or of precedents hallowed by law—or more probably of both—the pope treats these signs of ecclesiastical power like facts that everyone can see with his own eyes, and in them he sees fulfillment of a prophecy of Jeremiah, which he gladly applies: "See, I have this day set thee over the nations and over the kingdoms."

It is particularly in unlawful situations that this hierarchical subordination is affirmed. There is in this something beyond the ranking of jurisdictions here below: civil power depends on the Church; and even in the Church, the lower depends on the higher; but the supreme authority depends only on God. For the Apostle has said that "the spiritual man is judge of all things and is himself subject to no man":

Therefore, if the earthly power errs, it may be judged by the spiritual power. But if the lesser spiritual power errs, it is judged by its superior; if the highest truly errs, it can be judged by God alone, not by man.

An immense privilege, one that places the pope in a sphere superior to the earth. In effect, this power has nothing human about it other than the person of its holder, but is, in reality, wholly divine since it was given and guaranteed to Peter and his successors by the very Son of God: "an authority . . . not human, but rather divine power, given by the divine word to Peter."

Nothing more remained to be done beyond drawing the conclusions called forth by these considerations. To resist a power ordained by God is to resist God Himself, unless one wants to revive Manichaean dualism. Furthermore, the same "necessity for salvation" that binds all men without exception to the Church equally imposes on them the strict duty of submission to the Roman Pontiff. Such is the doctrine that Boniface VIII sanctioned with every rigorous clause that characterized the acts of his supreme doctrinal magistracy:

Therefore whosoever resists this power so ordained by God resists the ordinance of God, unless he pretends there are two principles like a Manichean. . . . Whence we declare, say and define that it is altogether necessary for salvation that all human creatures be subject to the Roman pontiff.

The bull *Unam Sanctam* has been the object of passionate discussions among statesmen and theologians. While there have been a few rare panegyrists, it has found innumerable detractors. While our old Gallicans formerly experienced with it a vexation approaching scandal, Protestant polemicists rather took pleasure in it since it certainly gave them their heart's desire in supporting their prejudices or their rancor against pontifical absolutism. And on this point the situation sometimes appeared so difficult that embarrassed apologists could find nothing better, to cut short all the objections, than to deny the authenticity of the document. But they have had to bow to the evidence, especially the facsimile of the bull as it may still be read in the Register of Boniface VIII. Perhaps it is enough simply to understand it well: in any event, the historian has no other mission.

From the strictly theological point of view, the case presented in the bull *Unam Sanctam* contains nothing very disturbing, or even anything very special. One must only take care, in conformity with the rule of a rational exegesis, not to put all the propositions on the same level, not to transform arguments arising from the occasion or simple *obiter dicta* into official teachings. For it is an elementary principle of method that ecclesiastical authority—like any other—is bound only by the formal contents of its decisions. But here, as has been very rightly observed, the final clause, which alone carries the weight of the [doctrinal] definition, affirms nothing more than a general and absolutely indefinite duty of submission to the Roman pontiff: "It is altogether necessary for salvation . . . to be subject to the Roman pontiff." It is a definition that would perhaps be sufficiently safeguarded, if not in spirit at least in the letter, simply by understanding that spiritual power alone is meant, and the conclusion of the bull would thereby be bound to the dogmatic statements of the first part. Even supposing, as is probable, that one must take into account the political considerations developed in the middle and therefore that one must see in it a certain papal

claim in temporal matters, the fact remains that the formula of this right is strikingly discreet, something which makes it compatible with interpretations much more mild. Whatever the considerations may have been, they have not formally entered into the sentence. And this observation is decisive for anyone who is trained to move within the subtle jurisprudence of pontifical documents.

Besides, the strong personality of Boniface VIII and the boldness of his actions must not lead to a misunderstanding of the fact that his doctrine is, for the most part, fashioned from traditional elements. One finds, of course, nothing essentially new in the first half of the bull, which is pure dogma: the unity of the Church and the necessity of belonging to it in order to be saved were affirmed in formal terms . . . in the third century; the primacy of the Roman pontiff goes back in multiple strands to the oldest of ecclesiastical history. As for the powers of the Church whose exposition makes up the second part of the bull, not only the foundations, but even the wording is borrowed from older authors. . . .

The French response to *Unam Sanctam* was somewhat delayed, but violent. In March 1303 Philip summoned representatives from all three estates to central assemblies in which Boniface was roundly condemned; the king's new minister, William of Nogaret, was then dispatched to Italy "for certain business" pertaining to the crown. In June further meetings were held, and at one of them WILLIAM OF PLAISIANS (?–1313), another royal minister, presented the following formal charges of heresy against the pope. The scene was now set for the confrontation at Anagni.*

William of Plaisians

Charges of Heresy Against Boniface VIII

I, William of Plaisians, say, advance, and affirm that Boniface, who now occupies the Holy See, will be found a perfect heretic, according to the heresies, prodigious facts, and perverse doctrines hereafter mentioned:

1. He does not believe in the immortality or incorruptibility of the rational soul, but believes that the rational soul is corrupted along with the body.

2. He does not believe in the life eternal, . . . and he has not been ashamed to assert that he would rather be a dog, ass, or any other brute than a Frenchman, which he would not say if he believed that a Frenchman had a soul. . . .

4. He does not faithfully believe that, because of the words instituted by Christ, spoken by a faithful and ordained priest over a Host in the way set by the Church, it becomes the true body of Christ. . . .

6. He is reported to claim that fornication is no more a sin than is rubbing one's hands together: and this he has said loudly and publicly.

7. He has often said that if nothing else could be done to humble the king and the French, he would ruin himself, the whole world, and the whole Church. . . .

9. To perpetuate his most damnable memory he has had silver statues of himself erected in churches, in this way leading men into idolatry.

10. He has a private demon whose advice he follows in all things. Whence he has once said that if all the men in the

*From Pierre Dupuy, *Histoire du différend d'entre le pape Boniface VIII et Philippes le Bel, roy de France* (Paris, 1655), pp. 102–106. Translated by G. H. Smith and Charles T. Wood.

world were on one side and he on the other, they could not deceive him, either in law or in deed, which is impossible unless he employs the demonic art. And all this is publicly known.

11. He is a soothsayer who consults diviners and oracles. And all this is publicly known.

12. He has publicly preached that the Roman pontiff cannot commit simony, which is heretical to say. . . .

14. Like a confirmed heretic, who claims the true faith as his alone, he has termed the French, notoriously a most Christian people, heretics. . . .

15. He is a Sodomite and keeps concubines. And this is publicly and commonly known.

16. He has had many clerks killed in his presence, rejoicing in their deaths. . . .

17. When he condemned a certain noble to prison, despite the latter's penitent pleas he forbade anyone to minister the sacrament of penance at the hour of death; from which it seems he believes that the sacrament of penance is not necessary for salvation.

18. He has compelled priests to violate the secrets of the confessional and, without the assent of those who confessed, has made their confessions public to their confusion and shame. . . .

19. He fasts neither on fast days nor in Lent. . . .

20. He has lowered and debased the status and rank of the cardinals, the black and white monks, and the Friars Minor and Preacher, often repeating that the world was being ruined by them, that they were false hypocrites, and that nothing good would happen to anyone who confessed to them. . . .

21. Seeking to destroy the faith, he has long harbored an aversion against the king of France, in hatred of the faith, because in France there is and ever was the splendor of the faith, the grand support and example of Christendom. . . .

23. It is notorious that the Holy Land has been lost as a result of his sins. . . .

24. He is openly termed a simonist, indeed the font and source of simony, selling benefices to the highest bidder, imposing on the Church and bishops both serfdom and the *taille,* so that he may enrich his family and friends with the patrimony of the Crucified and make them marquises, counts, and barons. . . .

25. It is notorious that he has dissolved many legitimately consummated marriages against the precept of the Lord and to the hurt and scandal of many; and he raised to the cardinalate his married nephew, a man wholly unworthy and inexperienced, one who led and leads a notoriously dissolute life, while his wife was alive. . . . And all this is publicly known.[1]

26. It is notorious that he treated his predecessor Celestine inhumanely, a man of holy memory who led a holy life; and that, because Celestine could not resign and because, therefore, Boniface could not legitimately succeed to the Holy See, the latter threw him in prison and had him quickly and secretly killed. And all this is widely and publicly known by the whole world. . . .

29. It is notorious that he seeks not the salvation of souls, but their perdition.

---

[1] The basis for this charge is discussed by Fawtier in the second-following article; the validity of most of the other charges is analyzed by Powicke in the final selection. — *Ed.*

In his treatment of Anagni, T. S. R. BOASE has taken the opportunity to mention some of Boniface's achievements which are frequently overlooked by the historians of his reign. In so doing, he gives new dignity to the outraged pope. This approach allows him at the same time to argue effectively against some of the wilder versions of Boniface's last moments.*

T. S. R. Boase

Boniface VIII:
A Peaceful Man at the End

Anagni stands above the broad valley of the Sacco, an irregular outline of rooftops on the lower ridge of Monte San Giorgio. Beyond, the Ernican hills rise more steeply, with small, speckled villages, Acuto, Piglio, half rocks, half buildings. To the south-east the road winds over rising country to Ferentino, clearly visible on its northern slope; and opposite, Sgurgola clambers along an outlying spur of the Lepine mountains, below the ancient walls of Segni, in whose church Alexander III canonised Becket, and sanctified the cause for which he died. To the north, beyond the tower of Piombinara, that still stands perilously on its cloven base, the valley widens towards Rome. Boniface could look out, over the brown and green of its summer distance, towards the ruined hill-top of Palestrina.

He had done much for his native city. Its podestà had much independence, though the rectorate of the Campagna and Maritime was as fully organised as any in papal territory. When the rector sought to intervene over some corpse found in the highway by the city, the commune successfully vindicated its right to the rare privilege of guarding its own roads, and collecting its own tallage for the purpose. Boniface liked the compromise of balanced powers; rectors, communes, family influence all played their part in his scheme of local government; and at Anagni on 6 September, the very eve of the outrage, he issued his last and curious

*From T. S. R. Boase, *Boniface VIII* (London: Constable & Company Ltd., 1933), pp. 341–351. Footnotes omitted.

edict for rule in the *dominium,* the code for the Mark of Ancona. . . .

It was in those last months also that Boniface bestowed a mark of special favour upon Rome. Before the violent end there is a pause, a period of quiet: while in France they plotted Nogaret's coup, and drew up the list of papal vices, Boniface legislated for the advancement of sound learning. On 20 April, 1303, he issued a bull setting up a university for the city. Hitherto Rome had had no *studium generale:* there had been, since Innocent IV's time, a *studium curiae* for training papal servants in legal practice;[1] but it was a specialised body, which could never achieve Boniface's aim that "the city to which God had given so many good gifts should become famous for learning." This partial *studium* seemed very narrow to the former scholar of Bologna. Boniface regarded learning, particularly legal, with a broad and tolerant outlook. He was anxious that civil law should be studied as well as canon law; it was "opportune and useful" to know something of this subject which nourished so many of his chief opponents. It was impossible to have compiled the Sext without keen realisation of the importance of learned centres both for reference and for criticism. One of Boniface's earliest orders had been for the cataloguing of the papal library, and he had added considerably to it, particularly with regard to legal commentaries, while his collection of thirty-three works in Greek, the largest western collection known at this period, suggests an interest in learning of a deeper, less vocational type. So the new university was given full privileges, and though its existence was soon to be cut

short, it was to revive again after the years of the captivity and the schism were over.

Rome was not Boniface's only academic interest. In 1295 when he made Pamiers a bishopric, he had also granted it a *studium generale,* though there had been little chance for any such peaceful developments there. In Aragon and Castile he had urged the kings to aid Lerida and Salamanca: in France he had intervened both at Paris and Orleans. But Paris, leader of all universities, did not love him. He had dealt roundly with some of its masters at that ill-fated synod of Ste. Geneviève: many of them had argued that Celestine's renunciation was illegal: but not all: even in Paris, in the crisis of 1303, only a majority opinion, no general consent, could be obtained for Philip's support. With Oxford, far less powerful than Paris, relations had been more friendly. The university sought the privilege *ubique docendi,*[2] that Oxford graduates, along with those of Paris and Bologna, might be entitled to lecture anywhere. Boniface gave no final decision on this question, but he freed the university from all episcopal intervention and placed it completely under the jurisdiction of its chancellor. On lesser matters also he was prepared to protect it, and in 1302 defended the endowments of Merton College. Finally, a strangely prophetic act, in July 1303 Boniface raised the School at Avignon to the status of a *studium generale.* It is a bull which contains passages of writing where strong feeling breaks through conventional phraseology; and Boniface's praise of Latin study, as the meeting-place of all nations, the *lingua franca* which leads to peace and understanding, reveals a perception of his high office which is sometimes lacking

---

[1] A *studium generale* was a school for general studies, a university where all the seven liberal arts were studied; a *studium curiae* was a more specialized institution, concentrating on law. — *Ed.*

[2] A *ubique docendi* was an ecclesiastical license to teach, granted by the pope and valid throughout Western Christendom. — *Ed.*

in the arguments of more controversial matters.

Avignon's greatness was to come. Anagni's was passing. The hill town that had bred so many popes was to become a village under a curse, left without power of growth, overburdened by memories. The early frescoed art of its cathedral, the rich stuffs Boniface had brought there, the palace Gregory IX had built, the newer houses of the Caetani, these were to remain, slowly decaying: they were to have no successors. Eleven Anagniotes held bishoprics under Boniface; the town gave rectors to all the Patrimony, its citizens drew incomes from canonries all over Europe. Leonard, Bishop of Anagni, was a man "long known to the pope," a trusted collector of papal tenths, who readily obtained privileges from the Holy See. But the days of this prosperity were all but over.

It was on 6 September, 1303, that Nogaret and his fellow-conspirators met at Ferentino, riding in separately with small bands of followers. They were all men with grievances, real or imagined, against Boniface: Sciarra Colonna with a troop of horse; Rainald of Supino, whose sister Maria had been divorced by Francis Caetani; his son Robert and his his brother Thomas of Morolo; Nicholas Conti, whose family had been dispossessed of Sgurgola; two of the Ceccano, relatives of the rebel John, who still lay in a papal prison; Peter Colonna of Genazzano and his son Stephen, pensioners of the court of France; Peter of Lupara and his son Orlando, Neapolitan knights; Maximus of Trevi; such were the "servants of faction" who had so fiercely taken up arms. Inside the town they had allies, Adenulf *di papa*, brother of Nicholas Conti, and Godfrey Bussa, the commander of the papal guard. Early on the morning of the 7th, while it was still dark,

they came from Ferentino, by a path up the eastern slope of the hill to the Porta Tufoli. To-day there are only fragments of the gate: the great houses there are crumbling, inhabited by many families, with lanes cut through their courtyards; and the old path up to the gateway loses itself amongst hen-runs and vegetable plots. But in that September there were firm walls and defences: it was by treachery that the gate was left open for the conspirators to enter, with the standards of the church and of France, some 300 horse and 1,000 foot. They were mainly local levies: the only French were Nogaret and two servants.

There was soon noise in the narrow streets. The terror of sudden awakening lives on in William Hundleby's account[3] which he sent back to the good folk in Lincoln of all these foreign doings. "Men and women were leaping from their beds and opening the doors, asking the cause of such hubbub, and it was discovered that Sciarra Colonna, brother of the condemned cardinal, had entered the town with a great power acquired through the King of France that he might seize the pope and give him to death." The bells clanged out, and the people rushed to the market-place: Adenulf *di Papa* was chosen as their captain, a move probably prepared in advance, by working on minor grievances readily incidental to the papal residence in the town. The citizens were carried away by the thrill of the moment and welcomed the conspirators: Godfrey Bussa with many of the papal guard joined them. In the lower part of the town and on the eastern slope by the Porta Tufoli they plundered the houses of the cardinals. In the dark, steep alleys there

---

[3] Hundleby was an English cleric whose account of the events at Anagni is generally regarded as the most reliable of those surviving.—*Ed.*

must have been wild confusion. There were not, that early September, many of the college present in Anagni. Matthew of Acquasparta had died in the preceding October: Gerard of Parma was dead: Matthew Rosso was in Rome, uneasy over the turn in Sicilian affairs: none of the pope's oldest friends was by him. Cardinal Gentile, Cardinal Francis Caetani, Cardinal Theodore of Orvieto made their escape. Napoleone Orsini and Richard of Siena were left unmolested, and it was common report that they had been in correspondence with the conspirators. Nicholas Boccasini and Peter of Spain were with Boniface in the papal palace.

Thither, while still early, six o'clock in the morning, the attack was concentrating. Boniface demanded what they sought; there was some negotiation and a truce till three in the afternoon. But the terms were that he should reinstate the Colonna, hand over all the treasure of the church to three senior cardinals, renounce the papacy and remain a prisoner. There was no possibility of accepting such conditions. At three o'clock the attack was renewed. But the papal palaces were strong, held desperately by a small body of faithful retainers: there were several casualties amongst the attackers: it seemed impossible to force the gates. The Caetani buildings held the crest of the town, blocking access to the small piazza of the cathedral, the highest point: a party detached itself from the attack, scrambled round the hill-side and climbed up on the south to the gate by the campanile. A crowd of papal supporters, clerks and laymen and merchants, had barricaded themselves in the cathedral. The rioters forced an entrance by firing the doors: there was plundering and some bloodshed. The Archbishop of Gran, who had escaped so many tumults, was killed by Orlando of Lupara at his father's orders. The grand-

father had died with Carrobert in Hungary:[4] perhaps there was some remote private vengeance to be exacted. And now from the cathedral side the palace of the Marquis could be attacked from the rear. Peter surrendered: he and his son Roffred were taken; the other son, Benedict, escaped by a privy. Across the narrow street (the further wall of his palace, buttressed on the hill-slope, gave no foothold for the invaders) the pope still held out: but when he learned of his nephew's capture, "he wept bitterly." Had all his planning come to this: that they should all die, and death seemed like enough, caught in a trap? There was little time for grieving. They had broken the windows and doors on the street side of his own palace. It was about six o'clock, the hour of vespers. Nogaret was with Marquis Peter when Sciarra and his men forced their way through to Boniface's chamber. Legend has been busy with this final moment and few chroniclers could resist some heightening of dramatic effect, so that the story grew how Boniface confronted his assailants, seated on the papal throne and holding the papal cross in his hands. That he had put on his papal robes seems certain: it was in keeping with his proud spirit to show him like a king. But the body was ageing, worn by strife and disease, bowed now by anxious affections and outraged pride. When the fierce shouts and jeers of the Colonna soldiery sank a little, and with Nogaret's hasty coming there was some peace in the room, the old man was lying on the couch, clasping the cross to his breast. So at least the frightened courtiers heard of it, or saw perhaps when some had courage to return to their master. For all had sought hiding:

---

[4] Carrobert was a son of Charles II of Sicily who conducted a long campaign to make good his somewhat tenuous claims to the throne of Hungary.—*Ed.*

only Peter of Spain had stayed by him to share his fate. Sciarra desired his enemy's death: when to his demands for resignation Boniface broke silence and affirmed the lawfulness of his pontificate, violence could hardly be restrained. Some believed the pope had been struck and roughly handled. "Here is my head, here is my breast," he said in the vernacular, and waited the end. But William Hundleby thought he had not been injured, and when Benedict XI said that "they laid hands upon him," he was already thinking of that divine parallel, whose aptness was to move even Dante's bitterness. Nogaret came, and the scandal of the pope's murder would have been fatal to his schemes. "What do you here, son of a Patarine?" said Boniface, and the words have the true ring about them, but Nogaret was in fact his protector. The pope was put under the guard of Rainald of Supino, as any common prisoner: "he might have been our Geoffrey Ceco or Peter Stall," wrote William to the people of Lincoln, "for all respect he got from them." "The Lord gave and the Lord has taken away": the old man sat muttering the words of Job: William's powers of description give out. "Et, ut creditur, Papa habuit malam noctem."[5]

Meanwhile there was division amongst the conspirators. Nogaret, with no troops of his own, could rely only on his personal influence. The invaders and the towns-people were out of hand. The papal treasury was broken into, and its great riches and works of art carried off by any who could lay hands on them. "No one could have believed that all the kings of the earth could have had such a treasure." The relics of the cathedral shared a like fate: the house of the Spini, the papal

bankers, was plundered. Everywhere cellars were ransacked, and the night became drunken.

Throughout the following day, when every moment was precious for his scheme of abduction—for soon some countermove must come—Nogaret argued with Sciarra, "Whether to kill the pope or bring him living to the King of France." News came that Sgurgola had driven out its Caetani garrison, that the Campagna was rising, but already several leading Anagniotes were saying that they could not allow the pope to be taken out of their city. Guarded in his room Boniface seemed sunk in apathy, refusing to eat. The long day wore on. On the Monday, several citizens met in secret. There had been a great revulsion of feeling. It needed but little instigation before the crowd was shouting for the pope's rescue. Probably some of the conspirators' troops joined them. There was renewed fighting. Nogaret was wounded, but both he and Sciarra escaped. Rainald of Supino and Adenulf were both captured. The pope was brought out from his prison and down to the market-place to absolve the people. With volatile enthusiasm the citizens trailed the French banner through the mud of their streets. Women brought gifts of wine and food. All was pity and indignation at the outrage. "And everyone could speak with the pope, as with any other poor man." In the evening Boniface again addressed the people, appealing for the restoration of the treasure, and now much of it was as readily disgorged as it had been plundered; much but not all.

The two suspected cardinals were pardoned, though they had confirmed their guilt by flight. Napoleone was to show in his long career an intriguing spirit that delighted in revolt. He himself later admitted that he had been in correspon-

---

[5] Holtzmann in *Festschrift*, p. 496, "And, as it is believed, the pope had a bad night."

dence with Philip, and was zealous against Boniface at the posthumous trial.[6] Richard had fled in his servant's clothes. Clear-headed and independent, he had remained a legal adviser whom the pope had often consulted: in April of the previous year he had nominated Henry of Cremona, the great upholder of papal supremacy, for the Bishopric of Reggio: in the process for Celestine's canonisation he, alone of all the cardinals, considered that no miracles were proven.[7] There are few opinions on Boniface that would be more worth the having than his, but reticence seems to have been part of his detached, sceptical character, and he has left no excuse nor explanation of his conduct.

A week later, on Monday, 16 September, Boniface left Anagni, under an Orsini escort sent from Rome. The Campagna was in great disturbance and Sciarra and his horse may even have attempted an attack. But on the 18th the pope reached his palace on the Lateran, and on the 21st he moved to the Vatican, where he was surrounded by the Orsini strongholds and protected by their power. Ferreto makes a story out of this move: that Boniface was blaming Charles of Naples for having allowed the attack on him to take place and was appealing to Frederick of Sicily;[8] which Matthew Orsini, Frederick's most constant opponent, would not countenance, and so the pope was held in captivity. But the story is obviously overstated: Charles wrote in horror at the news of the outrage, and there is no trace of any blame being put upon him: Sicilian negotiations had been for some time in progress: Matthew's one thought was to be "Vengeance for Anagni." It was for peace and security that the broken man crossed the river to the Vatican. No business was attempted: the brazen Peredo sought an audience on 6 October but was refused: "there is no hope," wrote Hundleby, "of any affairs being dealt with," and vowed his goods to the poor were he safely back in England. Poor fellow, he died in Rome before the year was out, and never saw Lincoln again.

A greater than he was dying: the pride that had been the motive force of every action was broken. They would not have it that Boniface died peacefully. He went mad, they said, gnashed his teeth, gnawed the flesh off his hands and dashed his brains out against the wall; while all his devils howled in a great storm and darkness around him. But his end was quiet, as all immediate accounts agree: he sank from weariness and exhaustion, and early on the morning of 12 October, about "the time of the first sleep," all was over.

When they opened his tomb in 1605, the body, well preserved, showed no signs of violence, the expression was one of calm resignation, and the hands were still complete and notably beautiful.

---

[6] After Boniface's death Philip continued his campaign against the late pope, bringing formal charges (particularly of heresy) before Clement V (1305–1314) for hearing. Clement found Philip's intent and actions "good and just" and ordered all of Boniface's offending bull publicly burned.—*Ed.*

[7] The canonization of Celestine was another aspect of Philip the Fair's continued attack on Boniface's memory. The canonization of his predecessor would naturally increase doubts about his own legitimacy as pope. Clement V, undoubtedly seeing this implication, was careful to canonize Celestine only as Pietro di Murrone, a private person, and not as pope.—*Ed.*

[8] Charles of Naples is Charles II of Sicily. Frederick of Sicily was the Aragonese claimant to the throne of the Two Sicilies; he had actual possession of the island, but not of the mainland.—*Ed.*

ROBERT FAWTIER (1885–1966) was for many years
the dean of French medievalists and a leading authority
on the growth of the Capetian monarchy. To
English-speaking readers he is best known for his
Capetian Kings of France, but scholars have long
appreciated his many articles, his studies (with
Ferdinand Lot) of the first French budget and of
medieval institutions, and particularly his editorship
of the documents of Philip the Fair. Because of this
work he came to know the materials of the reign better
than anyone else. In the following article he presents
a strikingly new and different interpretation of what
may have actually transpired at Anagni.*

Robert Fawtier

Nogaret and the Crime of Anagni

One of the difficulties that historians
encounter in studying the past lies in
assessing events at their true value. When
I say "true value," I mean the value attributed to them by contemporaries, the
only people directly affected. The crime
of Anagni provides an excellent example.

Textbooks agree that on September 7,
1303, at the order of King Philip the Fair
of France, William of Nogaret, a counselor of the king and a descendant of
heretics, entered the town of Anagni
where Pope Boniface VIII was staying
during his conflict with the French sovereign; Nogaret seized the pontiff's person, insulted him, had men from his own
escort strike him. Two days later, on
September 9, he had to flee in shame

when the town's inhabitants revolted
and freed the pope. . . .

The crime of Anagni occurred during
a period for which we have considerable
documentation, a time, indeed, when
kings and powers were accustomed to
keep themselves informed about developments in other courts through in-
quisitive and devoted agents. The court
of Rome, already in this period the cross-
roads of the world, was naturally a particularly valuable observation post, and
governments as well as certain private
businesses had observers there. Their
reports have survived, at least in part,
and it is curious to note that the rich and
thoroughly exploited Archives of Bar-
celona have offered no account of the

*From Robert Fawtier, "L'attentat d'Anagni," *Mélanges d'histoire et d'archéologie,* LX (1948), pp. 153,
155–162, 164–167, 169–179. Reprinted by permission of Mme Fawtier and of the École Française de Rome.
Translated by Charles T. Wood. Most footnotes omitted.

events of September 1303 from one of the agents maintained by the king of Aragon at the Curia. Equally astonishingly, the files of Ancient Correspondence in the Public Record Office at London reveal just as little about the assault on the pope. Lastly, it is curious that no Italian archive, public or private, has furnished us with any letter from the agents of the great Italian banks on these events.

It is difficult to imagine that systematic destruction could account for the disappearance of all memory of this sacrilege. The most reasonable explanation would appear to be that the importance of the event became apparent only much later and that, for contemporaries, it involved no more than a commonplace and fruitless attempt to kidnap the pope.

Although Dante in a famous triplet saw "Anagni by the Lilies taken, / And in His Vicar Christ a captive made," he wrote a number of years later; he was a poet; and it is not absolutely certain that in writing these lines he attached much importance to the event itself. One would be tempted to accept this view when one considers that Nogaret, the author of the assault, resides in none of the circles of Hell and that his coming there is nowhere foretold.

But what was Nogaret's role in this affair? . . . It is now very apparent that the only text on which we can genuinely rely to reconstruct these tragic days is the story of the English proctor [William Hundleby]. Moreover, his story inspires confidence; it is one of a poor man, very disturbed by the tumult prevailing in the Rome to which he returned with the pope. He takes no sides; he simply tells what he has seen. . . . But William Hundleby ignores William of Nogaret even though his story is extremely precise and reports the pope's own words. Would

this have been the case if Nogaret had played the role that history attributes to him, or could it be that history on this point is only legend?

We know from our Englishman that at dawn on September 7 a considerable body of men-at-arms both from "the king of France's party" and from that of the papally condemned Colonna cardinals appeared at the gates of Anagni, found them open, and entered the town. . . . William Hundleby remains properly vague about the assailants' numbers. He seems to discern two elements among them: partisans of the king of France and partisans of the Colonnas, but he makes no precise estimate concerning the respective strengths of the two groups.

In any event, the army entered Anagni and soon *(statim)* began to attack *(dare insultum)* both the pope's palace and that of his nephew Marquis Peter II Gaetani. This naturally caused some noise, which awakened the inhabitants of the town. Everyone, men and women alike, left their beds and opened their houses. They then learned that Sciarra Colonna, the brother of the condemned cardinals—actually, Cardinal Peter's brother and Cardinal James' nephew— had come with troops paid by the king of France "to seize the pope and to put him to death."

At this news the town bell began to sound and the population assembled and named a captain of the people, Adenulf de Mattia, called Adenulf di Papa, a great baron from the Campagna and a personal enemy of the pope, to whom the leaders of the people swore fealty and promised obedience in all things.

During this time, Sciarra was laying siege to the pope's palace, that of the marquis, and those of three cardinals: Gentile of Montefiore, cardinal of Saint Martin in montibus; Francis Gaetani, cardinal of Santa Maria in Cosmedin, nephew of Boniface VIII by his brother Roffred II; and Peter of Spain, cardinal-bishop of Sabina. Only the palaces of the cardinals were taken, and they themselves escaped through the latrines.

Then Adenulf di Papa arrived, the new captain of the people, accompanied by Rainald of Supino, also a great baron from the Campagna and a personal enemy of the pope. They brought with them the son of Lord "Johannes de Chican," apparently John of Ceccano, whom the pope had kept imprisoned since June 1299. This second wave of the assault was, so to speak, familial. Adenulf di Papa, of the great Conti family, was a relative of Boniface VIII, perhaps a nephew. Rainald of Supino's sister Maria had married Francis Gaetani, but "this fat young man," as Nogaret later called him, had obtained a divorce in 1295 when he was offered a cardinal's hat by his uncle. As for John of Ceccano, he too must have been related to the Gaetanis, Marquis Peter II's wife being one Joanna of Ceccano.

The arrival of these reinforcements convinced the pope and the marquis that they could not resist for long. "That is why the pope asked for a truce, which Sciarra granted both to him and the marquis until the ninth hour," the truce having begun at the first hour. Thus, from six o'clock in the morning until three in the afternoon, negotiations were held.

The pope first tried to win over the people of Anagni. They replied that they could do nothing without the consent of their captain. "The pope having heard this, messengers were sent hither and yon." Boniface VIII then had Sciarra asked what reparations he demanded for himself and his brothers. Sciarra replied that his life would be spared on three conditions: turning the treasure of the Church over to two or three of the oldest cardinals; making full reparation, spiritual and temporal, to the Colonna cardinals and their relatives; and, this having been done, renouncing the tiara and physically placing himself in the hands of the said Sciarra. William Hundleby adds that on hearing these conditions the pope said: "These words are hard." So negotiations continued.

But, at three in the afternoon, the truce expired and the assault began again. Since Anagni's cathedral stood in the way of the assailants' attack on the palaces of the pope and the marquis, Sciarra Colonna's men put its doors to the torch and entered the church, which they found full of "clerics, laymen, and merchants with knives and other saleable merchandise." They seized everything. At this, the marquis surrendered in return for a safe-conduct for him and his sons. The pope, learning of the surrender, shed bitter tears. Besides, his turn was about to come. The doors and windows of his palace, which alone continued to resist, were forced by fire, and the mob of assailants rushed in.

William Hundleby says that the pope's assailants covered him with threats and insults, threats and insults that he received in silence. When Boniface was asked if he wished to renounce the papacy, he refused, saying that he preferred to lose his head and remarking in Italian: *"Ecco l'collo, ecco l'capo,"* (Here is my neck, here is my head). On hearing this, Sciarra would gladly have killed him, but was prevented "by others." The English proctor further declares that "the pope received no bodily harm," but adds that he was abandoned by everyone save Cardinal Peter of Spain. Then Sciarra appointed guards for the pope and placed Rainald of Supino at their head. "And, as it is believed," our Englishman states, "the pope had a bad night." . . .

The pope remained captive until the following Monday (September 9). "During this time, Sciarra and his followers debated whether they should put the pope to death or send him living to the king of France." But the people of Anagni learned that the pope's life was in question. Alerted, they assembled secretly around nine o'clock Monday morning, without informing either their captain, Sciarra, or the other papal guards. Fearing for their city should the pope there be put to death, Anagni's inhabitants decided that they themselves should assure the protection of the pope and his nephews; if need be, they were prepared to put Sciarra and Boniface's guards to death if they offered any resistance. Having so decided, they, to the number of 10,000 armed men, drove Sciarra and his men from the city; many of the latter were killed; the pope and his nephews were rescued. This happened a little after three on Monday afternoon. . . .

So that is what an eyewitness, an impartial adherent of the Curia, wrote to an English prelate less than twenty days after the event. As we have seen, this tale leaves Nogaret no role. Does that mean he had none? Obviously not, and Nogaret's own admissions show us the contrary, but unfortunately no one has wanted to believe him until now. This legist has enjoyed a bad press: Catholic historians see him filled with impiety and sacrilege; liberal historians view him more or less as the head of Philip the Fair's Gestapo or Okrana.[1] Perhaps these current notions ought to be corrected, for this supposedly impious and sacrile-

gious man may well have had a soul that was religious to the point of fanaticism. A document discovered and published in 1917 by Charles-Victor Langlois throws new and strange light on this much discredited person. We have the original of this letter in Nogaret's own hand, addressed to Master Stephen of Suisy, a counselor of the king and later a cardinal. The letter is undated, but nevertheless contains enough evidence to fix its composition and dispatch with certainty to the first months of the year 1303.

Ill with fever, Nogaret found himself at Sens; about to leave on a trip, he first passed on to his correspondent a series of briefs on various affairs with which he had been entrusted by the king; he then added:

Fever delays me, my lord. . . . Please excuse me and know that you would not have had the other reports so quickly, had I been able to undertake the journey I had begun.

May the Lord by His grace direct your steps.

My lord, pray God that if my journey pleases Him, He may direct me in it. If it displeases Him, may He keep me from it by death or otherwise, at His pleasure.

The man who wrote these words appears to have realized that the mission he was undertaking might have grave consequences for religion, but it is also incontestable that he was profoundly religious. Yet Nogaret wrote this letter when he was starting the journey that was to end at Anagni.

It is commonly said that he went there on the king's orders, and we do in fact have the text of the commission given him. This commission, dated March 7, 1303, gave power to John Mouchet and William of Nogaret, knights, and to Masters Thierry d'Hirson and James of Jasseins, to repair "to certain regions for certain business" and there to negotiate in the king's name with all persons

---

[1] Respectively the secret police of Nazi Germany and tsarist Russia.—*Ed.*

of all parties, and to come to agreement with the said persons on all subsidies and subventions and to do, in a general way, everything they judged necessary for the king's service. Some have concluded from this wording that Philip the Fair dared not spell out the true motives for which his commission had been issued; the vagueness of the terms used seems Machiavellian. Yet it is enough just to peruse the tremendous number of commissions issued by Philip the Fair to realize that only current formulae are at stake, not anything unusual. . . .

But what does Nogaret himself tell us he went to do at Anagni? We know that he gave many and lengthy explanations of his role and that, in general, his depositions agree with each other even though they stretch out over a great many years. We should add that in many instances we have the original drafts written or corrected in his own hand. What does he say he did? There is one point on which he never varied; it is this: that the king had sent him to notify Boniface VIII of his summons to appear before the general council that the parlement "of the Realm," meeting at Paris, had decided to hold in order to judge or justify the pope. Nogaret had tried to meet the pope, to enter into negotiations with him. Boniface had not wanted to receive him, refused to begin relations with him. Then Nogaret learned that the pope was preparing a bull excommunicating the king of France; this bull, *Super Petri solio*, was to be promulgated on September 8, 1303.

No one has sufficiently noticed that so long as the pope failed personally to receive notification of the call to council, his acts would continue to bind all Christians. On the day he received notification, however, the value of these acts would undergo considerable change, for their validity would then depend on the decision arrived at by the council. If Nogaret was a fervent Christian, he was also a proctor who knew his job. Did he, therefore, take this summons accompanied by a considerable escort? Certainly not. He tells us himself that he was accompanied only by two squires. But he was the bearer of something infinitely more impressive: the symbols of royal majesty.

In an act of October 17, 1303, William of Nogaret assured Rainald of Supino, captain of Ferentino, of the king's protection, and in this document we find a most interesting bit of information. Nogaret informs us that after the about-face of the inhabitants of Anagni, they dragged through the streets of their town the *"vexillum ac insignia domini Regis"* (the banner and arms of the king). Another text . . . begins with these words: On September 7, 1303, before dawn, Lord William of Nogaret, *"portans vexillum et arma Philippi domini regis Francorum"* (carrying the banner and arms of Philip, lord king of France), entered Anagni. Thus Nogaret carried not only the royal banner, but also the royal arms. How should these latter words be taken? Doubt seems out of the question, for what were involved were escutcheons bearing the king's arms such as were placed on the frontiers, at the limits of those places which enjoyed royal protection.

Thus, the Parlement of the realm of France, meeting at Paris, had required the king of France to convoke a council before which Pope Boniface VIII would have to appear and justify himself; the latter was the accused; an appeal against him had been drawn up by the people of France. The king, charged by his people with the convocation of this council, had to assure protection for the accused. Once Nogaret had given the pope the citation convoking him, he would place the escutcheons bearing the arms of France at the four corners of the papal palace; he would have the banner of France raised over the roof of the palace; and, as the law dictated, the pope would thus be placed under the protection of the king of France until he had been judged.

But the pope's quarrels were not confined to the king of France. In Italy there were people who hated him cordially: the Colonnas and their partisans. I am very struck by the fact that when dealing with the group that entered Anagni, William Hundleby distinguishes between the men of "the king of France's party" and those of the Colonna cardinals' party. What was this group from "the king of France's party"? Obviously not just Nogaret and his two squires. Since we saw that Rainald of Supino, captain of Ferentino, appeared fairly rapidly on the scene and since, on the other hand, we saw that on October 17 Nogaret assured the same Rainald of the king of France's eventual protection and declared that the captain of Ferentino had accompanied him to Anagni, we conclude that "the king of France's party" was represented in the group that presented itself at the gates of Anagni by Nogaret, his two squires, and Rainald of Supino. But, as we noted above, when Rainald of Supino intervened, he was accompanied by the new captain of Anagni, Adenulf di Papa, and by the son of John of Ceccano, and we underlined the family relationships that bound these people to the pope. Since the king of France's envoy came almost alone, he had relatives of the pope escort him so that he could present the summons.

But he was accompanied by others too. We have seen that as soon as the group entered Anagni, the people of the city were summoned by the pealing bell to the main square; there they elected a captain whom everyone swore to obey. The bearer of royal coercion was escorted as much by the representatives of one of the Holy See's cities, by true members of the Roman Church, as by the pope's family. Thus we can see what the anticipated plan had been: Nogaret would come to present his summons, to place his banner and escutcheons; the pope's relatives and the inhabitants of Anagni, his children and fellow countrymen, would assure safekeeping for the accused under the supreme protection of the king of France. This would have been a perfectly regular procedure; but one senses just the same why a man as religious as Nogaret would have had scruples about undertaking this task and why he would have left to God the question of preventing him from doing it or letting him accomplish it.

Unfortunately, there was one factor on which he had not counted: the Colonnas. It is apparent that the arrival of Nogaret and the men from Ferentino was expected at Anagni. Were we not told that they found the gates open? The way in which the people of Anagni welcomed the invaders—without fear, opening their doors and windows instead of closing them, assembling on the square when the bell sounded, electing a captain without, it seems, much discussion—all this leaves no doubt that the *coup* was planned and that the city knew what was going to happen. Were we not also told that the merchants had placed their pillaged merchandise in the cathedral? This precaution certainly indicates that the merchants knew the risks they might have to run. If the merchants of Anagni, if a good part of the population, were informed, certainly the Colonnas could have learned. The revolt that broke out in the patrimony of the Church and in the Campagna immediately after the pope's arrest indicates that there was an organized movement everywhere. This movement was manifestly related to Nogaret's actions, but it does not follow that he was its author. If . . . Mgr. Mouche was playing a role in this affair, it is more reasonable to suppose that this political movement ought to be attributed to him. The Colonnas knew, therefore, what was being plotted, no matter how they were informed.

Summoned or not, they appeared at the rendezvous in front of Anagni's gates. If they were not the first to enter, they immediately caught up with "the king of France's party," and Sciarra, their leader, immediately occupied himself with the pontifical treasure. All the legal trappings organized by Nogaret could not resist the passion of bandits from the Roman countryside, their appetite for pillage, and their family vendetta. But all this seems to have happened totally independently of Nogaret, for, to believe William Hundleby's testimony about it, the palaces of the three cardinals had been taken and the pope's already besieged when, in their turn, the people of Anagni arrived with Nogaret. Hundleby then speaks of an extended truce concluded between the adversaries and of the pope's long negotiations with Sciarra Colonna. Even there Nogaret's name does not arise. Incontestably, the Colonnas controlled the game from the beginning. But the Colonnas were not just pursuing political designs. They sought family vengeance and that is precisely how the pope understood it, for, as we have seen, the negotiations between him and the authors of the *coup de main* involved only the Colonnas and their affairs.

A little later William Hundleby tells us that when the pope was a prisoner, his captors discussed whether they should put him to death or send him to the king of France. This alone is enough to demonstrate that *the pope's kidnapping, his capture,* was in no way included among the king's projects and that the collusion with the Colonnas was, in this instance, a last-minute one imposed by the Colonnas on the king of France's representative. For it is most apparent that the king of France never wanted the pope's death. He was certainly prepared, if the council condemned the pope as a heretic, to lend the Church the strength of his secular arm and to bring Boniface VIII to the fire, but it never entered his head to have him assassinated.

The story told by Peter of Parroy, prior of "Chesa," is well known. When the king was preparing to send him to Italy and Rome in order to proclaim the appeal to the council, a great prelate, one who sat on the king's council, said to him: "Prior, thou knowest what a wicked and heretical man Boniface is, and how many evils and scandals he has already caused, and how many worse yet he will cause if he lives. I therefore tell thee that, in good conscience, in my opinion, thou wouldst be doing a meritorious deed if thou wert to kill him. And kill him calmly at the risk of my soul." To this the king made personal reply: "He shall not do it, please God, because the prior could become bishop or pope. But go, prior, and do what you have been enjoined to do and as it has been enjoined to you by these two prelates of my council whom you know, and who are faithful, informed, and constant." Besides, everyone agrees on this point: even Philip the Fair's most bitter enemies have never thought to accuse him of so black a design. The whole violent side of the affair came from the Colonnas, and the king's indignation when he learned what had happened[2]—

[2] Deposition of Cardinal Nicholas of Fréauville, O.P., former confessor of the king, at Avignon,

when he said, he too, that he had not wanted it—is certainly an expression of sincere feeling.

We think, therefore, that the affair at Anagni completely changed its complexion as a result of the Colonnas. The procedurally correct presentation of a summons to the general council became the occasion for scuffling in which a group of barons from the Campagna attempted to satisfy a vendetta.

It seems likely that contemporaries viewed it this way. It seems likely also that Pope Benedict XI, an eyewitness of the events, may have understood it this way. We know, in fact, that on June 7, 1304, this pontiff promulgated the bull *Flagitiosum Scelus,* in which the assailants were convoked to Perugia on the day of the Holy Apostles (June 29). They were there to appear before the pope to hear their sentence, one about which there could be no doubt since the pope referred to the accused as "those sons of perdition, eldest sons of Satan, nourished by perversity" who, "having cast aside all shame, having rejected all reverence—that of the subject for the prelate, of the son for the father, of the vassal for his lord—horribly and injuriously seized Pope Boniface at Anagni and laid impious hands on him." There followed sixteen names, of which the first was that of William of Nogaret.

More than anything else, it is *Flagitiosum Scelus* that has helped give the crime of Anagni its exaggerated place in history. It should be noted that when it was promulgated, Pope Benedict XI had already absolved the king of France

---

April 14, 1311. . . . : "In truth, concerning the capture of Lord Boniface I know and say nothing, except that the lord king neither approved it, nor commanded it, nor ordered it to be done; on the contrary, when he heard of it, he was at first greatly stupefied and, in speaking to me about it at that time, he said that it was a strange and horrible deed. . . . "

with regard to any accusation, since on March 25 the pope had relieved the king of France of every sentence of excommunication that he could have incurred; and, further, since on April 18 from Viterbo, on April 22 from Bolsena, on May 13 from Perugia, Benedict XI had annulled every sentence placed by Boniface VIII on the king, his agents, and the clerics of the realm. All the old favors were reestablished; a tenth for two years, annates for three, were conceded to the king, whose wife, brother, and family received numerous privileges. Only Nogaret was excluded. Understandably he was embittered, and understandably he then undertook his extraordinary campaign in search of personal vindication of his innocence. One can believe that Pope Clement V, who finally ended the affair, came to realize perfectly well what Nogaret's role had been. For while it is generally known that Clement condemned him to various pilgrimages he never made, what is less known is that on May 11, 1312, William of Nogaret received the privilege of having a portable altar and of having mass said on it every day, the same privilege being equally granted to William of Plaisians, Nogaret's co-worker in this whole affair, save at Anagni.

What, then, actually happened? At a time when pontifical centralization and the Sovereign Pontiff's infallibility had not, as yet, profoundly transformed the attitude of Catholics toward their vicar, a pope appeared whose orthodoxy and legitimacy appeared rightly or wrongly suspect. Therefore his case had to be submitted to higher authority in the form of the Church assembled in council. In order for this council to take place and for the accused to appear before it, he had to receive a citation to appear. Given the status of the accused, this citation was brought to him by a counselor of the king of France, promoter of the council. In order to be able to get as far as the pontifical palace, to leave the citation there, to have the king's escutcheons planted there, Nogaret had troops accompany him, men-at-arms from the city of Ferentino commanded by Rainald of Supino. He had also entered into relations with the inhabitants of Anagni, but he arrived almost alone, accompanied only by two squires. These negotiations, these preparations, became known, and the Colonnas decided to take advantage of the affair to settle an old debt. They appeared at the rendezvous. Nogaret entered the town; the population, unhappy with the pope, took advantage of this entry to carry out its little municipal revolution. But while everyone was assembled at the square to elect a captain, while Nogaret and Rainald of Supino were getting organized before proceeding to the pontifical palace for which the dwellings of the pope's relatives served as advanced defenses (relatives who, having profited from Boniface's elevation, bore no hostility toward him), the Colonnas seized the initiative and immediately gave this simple procedural measure a character of savage violence. Nogaret did what he could. He succeeded in saving Boniface's life. Two days later, an about-face of Anagni's inhabitants drove out Nogaret, the Colonnas, and the men-at-arms from Ferentino, thus definitively reestablishing the *status quo*.

For contemporaries, Anagni was an incident without importance, a *coup de main* infinitely less important than the carrying off of the Church's treasure by the Colonnas on May 3, 1297. That is why no one spoke of it. It was only Nogaret's pleas for rehabilitation and the obstinacy of the Holy See in heaping multiple responsibilities on a single man that gave this event its importance. It became a kind of symbol of the battle between spiritual and temporal, and people no longer understood what had actually happened. Under the impact of passing years and of different political, ideological, and literary inventions, it has even finally become a truly major fact of history.

What sort of man was Philip the Fair? What did he
hope to achieve in his struggles with Boniface VIII?
Was he, indeed, the master of his government's
policies? These are questions that have long troubled
historians, for in some measure one's sense of the
significance of the struggle—not just for France, but
for all secular governments—depends on one's view
of the king and his aims. In the following selection
CHARLES-VICTOR LANGLOIS gives his opinion.*

Charles-Victor Langlois

Philip the Fair: The Unknown King

In writings contemporaneous with
Philip the Fair and his sons, there is
nothing, or almost nothing, about the
personality of the kings. We must, therefore, resign ourselves: one will never
know who Philip the Fair was. It will
always be impossible to decide between
those who say "He was a great man" and
those who say "He let everything go."
This little problem is insoluble.

The sources from which we may gain
an idea of a person are his writings, and
accounts by people who have known
him or who without having known him
have undertaken to gather together the
echoes of public rumor.

The letters of Philip the Fair and of
his sons may be counted by the thousands. The temptation is great to compile
phrases from them—some of them are
sonorous—and to attribute to Philip or
to his sons the sentiments that the phrases
express. But one must resist the temptation, for in this era the letters and in-
structions sent from the royal chanceries
in the name of the kings were not dictated
by them. They were drawn up by notaries,
and the greater part of the general considerations in them are mere hallowed
formulas. Some few of them, it is true,
have a special flavor, but there is no justification for thinking that the prince was
the author, or even the inspirer, of the
rare pieces whose style is truly original.
We have no way of distinguishing what
originated with the king and what with

*From Charles-Victor Langlois, *Saint Louis—Philippe le Bel: Les derniers Capétiens directs,* volume
III² of Ernest Lavisse, *Histoire de France* (Paris, 1902), pp. 119–122. Reprinted by permission of Librairie
Hachette et Cie., Paris. Translated by Charles T. Wood. Footnotes omitted.

his ministers. In short, from the present point of view, nothing can be done with diplomatic documents.

Neither Philip the Fair nor his sons had a Joinville;[1] none of the men who were in regular contact with them recorded their sayings, their actions, or their deeds. Alone, among his counselors, William of Nogaret left a sketch about Philip the Fair, but it is a pompous fragment, apologetic, oratorical, and vague:

"My lord the king," he says in one of the memoirs written apropos of the affair with Boniface, "is of the race of the kings of France who all, since the time of King Pepin, have been religious, fervent champions of the faith, vigorous defenders of Holy Mother Church. . . . He has been, before, during, and after his marriage, chaste, humble, modest in bearing and language; he never gets angry; he hates no one; he envies no one; he loves everybody. Full of grace and love, pious, merciful, always following the path of truth and justice, slander is foreign to him. Fervent in the faith, religious in his life, building churches, practicing works of piety, handsome and charming in countenance, agreeable to all, even to his enemies when they are in his presence, God brings miraculous cures to the sick through his hands."

A few short accounts are given by people who saw the last Capetians of the direct line with their own eyes, but they are of little interest. One of the witnesses in the trial of Bernard Saisset, Bishop of Pamiers, reported that the bishop, speaking of Philip the Fair, said, "Our king resembles an owl, the fairest of birds, but worthless. He is the handsomest man in the world, but he only knows how to look at people unblinkingly, without speaking." The bishop is supposed to have added, "He is neither a man nor a beast; he is a statue." The Tuscan Francesco da Barberino, who was in France on business from 1309 to 1313, was struck by the affability of the king of France, who one day in his presence returned the salutation of three vile merrymakers *(vilissimi ribaldi),* let them approach him, and patiently listened to their grievances. Yves, a monk from St. Denis who was present during Philip's last moments, has described his devout end, similar to every devout end. Like St. Louis, Philip the Fair, although dying, would have refused to take a little mulled egg because it was a fast day. He would have spoken some edifying words; he would have exhorted his eldest son to love God, to revere the Church, to defend it, to be diligent in the divine offices, to surround himself with good men, to dress modestly. He would also have expressed some "sad reflections," a sign of great banality, "on the emptiness of human grandeur." This same monk dared to sketch a full-length portrait of the king he had seen die but whom he knew only slightly; his tame and mawkish epithets do not teach us much.

"This king," he says, "was very handsome, sufficiently literate, affable in countenance, very seemly in manner, humble, gentle, too humble, too gentle, precise in the performance of the divine offices. He fled evil conversations. He observed the fast; he wore a hair shirt; he accustomed himself to the administration of discipline by his confessor, with a little chain, *cum quadam catenula.* Simple and benevolent, he believed that everyone was moved by good intentions; that made him too trusting; his advisers took advantage of him."

Every other bit of information to be found in the chronicles, contemporary or later, is popular hearsay. It has value only as an indication of what the public thought.

---

[1] Friend and biographer of Louis IX (1226–1270), who was canonized in 1297.—*Ed.*

The contemporaries of Philip the Fair believed, if we may judge by the similar affirmations of Villani, Geoffrey of Paris, and many anonymous writers, that the king had a weak character. The interpolater of the romance *Fauvel,* who does not have "the merit of originality" although some have claimed it for him, has described the king as "easygoing." All agreed that he was handsome, fair skinned, blond haired, tall and strong, and "full of goodness, gentleness, and rectitude," and that he blindly let himself be led by those who had gained his confidence. In a Latin diatribe that dates from the first years of the reign, an anonymous writer accuses him of being intemperate, excessively fond of hunting, and surrounded by "villains," traitors, robbers, and impudent men; these the king obeyed *(quasi servus obedit),* and he neglected his duties. Geoffrey of Paris, the Parisian newsmonger whose work begins in 1300, could not write enough on this theme. Our king, he says, is an apathetic man, a "falcon"; while the Flemings acted, he passed his time in hunting. . . . He is a child; he does not see that he is being duped and taken advantage of by his entourage. . . . After the disaster of Courtrai, new admonitions: the indolence, the extreme feebleness of Philip toward his bad counselors, of low birth, were again denounced. . . . Later, the author of a piece entitled *A Dream* summed up the reign of Philip IV: it was a time when one hunted. . . .

Many texts confirm the preceding; there is none that contradicts them. If Philip the Fair passed as an energetic and attentive man among his contemporaries, this opinion has left no trace.

JOSEPH R. STRAYER (b. 1904) is Dayton-Stockton
Professor of History at Princeton University and a
former president of the Mediaeval Academy of
America. A French specialist, he has long pondered
the question of Philip's responsibility for the actions
of his government, and the difficulty of the issues
involved is nowhere better illustrated than in the
gradual development of his views. In 1939, for example,
when the problem was only secondary to his real
scholarly concerns, he nevertheless remarked: "I feel,
at present, that Philip had little control over his
ministers and that many important acts represent the
desires of the bureaucracy rather than those of the
king." By 1956, however, when the following article
appeared, he had totally changed his mind.*

Joseph R. Strayer

Philip the Fair: A "Constitutional" King

I

The reign of Philip the Fair offers one of the great paradoxes of French history. On the one hand, it sees the culmination of the medieval French monarchy; the royal government reaches a peak of power which it is not to attain again for generations. On the other hand, the king who presides over the government during these crowded years of great events is a shadowy, elusive figure, almost completely hidden behind a screen of bureaucrats. It is hard to prove that any important act of the reign was the result of a personal decision by the king. It is easy to argue that he did nothing, and by doing nothing allowed his ministers to express the traditions of the bureaucracy in a relentless drive for power. And yet those who believe that the important decisions of the reign were made by Philip's ministers merely change the form but not the substance of the paradox. For no one minister held power throughout the reign and no one minister had complete control of the government for even a short period. Yet basic policy remained constant, though tactics changed. If the king did not give continuity and direction to policy, who did? Can it be true that the whole bureaucracy was so imbued

*From Joseph R. Strayer, "Philip the Fair—A 'Constitutional' King," *American Historical Review,* LXII (1956), pp. 18–27, 29–32. Reprinted by permission of Joseph R. Strayer, Princeton University. Some footnotes have been omitted, and the Latin and French quotations in those remaining have been translated by Charles T. Wood. The quotation in the headnote is from Joseph R. Strayer and Charles H. Taylor, *Studies in Early French Taxation* (Cambridge, Mass., 1939), p. 4, note 2.

with the spirit of aggrandizement that it made no difference who was selected to sit in the royal Council? Or did Philip express his hidden desires through a careful choice of ministers?

This problem worried Philip's contemporaries, and it has worried historians ever since. On the whole, French writers of the early fourteenth century tended to believe that Philip was dominated by civil counsellors. This is the story of Yves of St. Denis, of Geoffroi de Paris, even of such an ardent supporter of the monarchy as Pierre Dubois. Bishop Bernard Saisset made many indiscreet remarks, but the one which stung most and has been remembered longest was his comparison of Philip to the owl: "the handsomest of birds which is worth absolutely nothing . . . such is our king of France who is the handsomest man in the world and who can do nothing except to stare at men."[1] Foreign chroniclers such as the Italian Villani and the Fleming Gilles le Muisis also believed that Philip was a figurehead. Even Boniface VIII, in listing Philip's offenses in *Ausculta fili*, thought it wise to insert some lines attacking the king's evil counsellors, though he added that this was no excuse and that the king bore full responsibility for allowing such men to have power.[2] The Aragonese writer who said that Philip was a masterful ruler, emperor, pope, and king rolled into one, was an exception.

Modern historians have been less willing to write Philip off as a nonentity. The Germans, who see Philip as the originator of the French drive to the east, are especially emphatic on this point. . . . The English historian Boase warns against "believing that so much of France was created . . . with no central guiding will." French scholars, who should know the facts best, are a little less sure. Boutaric believed in Philip's leadership and personal responsibility, but Boutaric wrote at the very beginning of serious scholarly investigation of the period. Langlois felt that the problem was insoluble, but his discussion does not do much to convince the reader that Philip was a strong king. Digard, without taking a very definite stand, tended to ascribe responsibility to the "counsellors of the king," to the "court," to Pierre Flote, rather than to Philip. On the other hand Fawtier, who knows the documents of the reign better than any other historian, has no doubt that Philip controlled and directed his government. He admits that some measures may have been initiated by members of the Council rather than by the king, but he is sure that Philip always knew and approved what was done in his name.[3]

More opinions on both sides of the question could be found, but this is not a problem which can be settled by accumulating authorities. Medieval chroniclers are not very reliable on such matters; many were ill-informed and all were influenced by the convention which blamed unpopular acts of kings on evil advisers. Modern writers are better informed, but are sometimes misled by other conventions: that the great events of a reign must be the result of deliberate

---

[1] Pierre Dupuy, *Histoire du différend d'entre le pape Boniface VIII et Philippes le Bel* (Paris, 1655), p. 643. That the simile hurt is shown by the fact that it is mentioned several times in royal documents dealing with the bishop's imprisonment. *Ibid.,* pp. 656, 660.

[2] Dupuy, p. 51. Boniface, like the chroniclers, suggests that the king's agents are feathering their own nests and that they use royal authority to oppress the people.

[3] For additional information on the historians here named, see Suggestions for Further Reading. —*Ed.*

policy, and that such a policy can be imposed only by a king. In all the discussion there has been too much arguing from effect to cause, too much concentration on a few striking, and therefore exceptional, events. It may be worth shifting ground for a moment and approaching the problem from another angle, that of the normal, routine activity of the French government. If we find that the king took an active part in dull, routine work, we shall be less willing to admit that he was passive in greater matters. Moreover, small decisions have a way of adding up into major policies, and Philip could easily have set the tone of the entire government through acts which made no great impression on envoys or chroniclers.

We can begin by admitting that many things were done in the king's name about which he knew nothing. France was a large country and had, even then, an unusually high density of bureaucrats, both at Paris and in the provinces. Most of these bureaucrats were trying to distinguish themselves by ceaseless activity in preserving, discovering, and increasing royal rights and revenues. Within certain limits, they had a free hand; they did not have to go to the king for authority for each act, and they received few specific orders regarding their ordinary work.

Yet there were limits, and these limits became apparent whenever a provincial official tried to go too far or too fast in his task of increasing royal power. The government of Philip the Fair was not very tender of the rights of bishops or of communes, but it had more respect for these rights than many local officials. It preferred to hold at least to the letter of the law; it would rather restrict than abolish privileges. It also knew that certain bishops were influential enough to need careful handling and that the loyalty

of certain provinces (especially in the South) was too uncertain to stand much rough treatment. Therefore we have dozens of letters forbidding royal officials to trouble bishops such as Guillaume le Maire of Angers, or communes such as that of Toulouse. Some of these letters are so emphatic and so personal that it is hard to believe that anyone could have written them except the king himself. Certainly no ordinary royal official could have threatened a seneschal of Périgord with severe punishment for failure to observe the rights of the consuls of Cahors,[4] or told a *bailli* of Caen that his goods would be confiscated if justice were not done to a king's clerk. And the king seems personally concerned when he rebukes a seneschal of Carcassonne for summoning men for military service, not only without a royal order but against a specific order: "such acts," says Philip, "will gain us the ill-will and hatred of our subjects."[5]

It is, of course, impossible to prove conclusively that these letters were written by direct order of the king. But it is clear that there was an inner circle in the government which had full control over all other royal officials and which insisted that its policies should be carried out at all levels of administration. The character of Philip's reign was not determined by a blind drive for power by a horde of petty bureaucrats. Policy was made at the high-

---

[4] Archives Nationales, J341, no. 8. The king is especially angry because earlier letters for Cahors have been "scorned" (March, 1308).

[5] Claude Devic and Joseph Vaissete, *Histoire générale de Languedoc,* new edition by Auguste Molinier and others (Toulouse, 1872–1905), X, *preuves,* col. 236. It is especially striking that this strong letter of March 11, 1289, was followed (col. 238) on September 17 by a much milder one allowing the seneschal to demand service in case of necessity. Certainly someone in Paris had been worrying about the case.

est level by a very few men, by the king and his Council.

Accepting this, one can still argue that the king was the least important member of the governing group, that he merely ratified decisions which were made by the Council as a whole, or by some of its leading members. This hypothesis would seem to be strengthened, at first glance, by evidence that the king did not always know what members of the Council did in his name. From time to time we hear of letters which have been obtained surreptitiously, of conflicting promises made by the king and members of the Council, of contradictory royal charters. But if these documents prove that the king did not always remember his promises or that he was not always informed of what was done in his name, they also prove that no one else was in complete control. In the competition for royal favors several men in succession might gain the king's ear; there was no single all-powerful favorite through whom patronage was channeled. Even more important, we hear of these contradictory orders because the king, in the long run, did become aware that his wishes were not being observed. And in every case he had his way; the surreptitious or conflicting letters were revoked; the claimant to whom the king really wished to give income or office received it. The only safe conclusion from this evidence is that there was some inefficiency, some failure of communication in the French government of the late thirteenth century. The same weaknesses are apparent in any other medieval government; they are not entirely absent in much more highly organized modern states.

Furthermore, someone in the government—almost certainly the king or the keeper of the seal—made an effort to prevent the appearance of these unauthorized or conflicting letters. The rule was gradually established that every document issued in the king's name must carry at the bottom the name of the notary who wrote it and the name of the official who ordered it written. The earliest examples of this practice which I have found come from the 1290's; by 1314 most documents are so authenticated. What is even more helpful to the historian is that the scribes who copied royal letters into the registers of the last years of the reign included in their copies the names of the notaries, and of the officials who ordered the letters written. This means that we have hundreds of cases in which we know precisely who took the responsibility for a certain act of government.

Most of the documents which appear in the registers deal only with trivial matters—such things as amortizations, approval of farms made by local officials, exchanges of property, gifts, acts of pardon and of grace. This has its advantages. We can be sure that we are watching the normal operations of government, not extraordinary procedures invented for great occasions. And it is at least a reasonable supposition that the men who work steadily on these routine matters will be well informed about the kingdom, well versed in administrative procedures, well acquainted with all important members of the court, and hence influential in making major decisions.

A rough tabulation of the names on these documents during the last five years of the reign yields interesting results. First of all, a rather large number of men —at least thirty-two—have authority to order letters written in the king's name. Not all of these men are very active; the great lords of the Council, men such as the counts of Valois and St. Pol, seldom command letters. On the other hand, there are about fifteen names which appear again and again. Purely numerical comparisons among this group would be meaningless, since the record is incomplete, and some letters are more important than others. It is clear, however, that there is a certain amount of specialization. For example, Philippe le Convers orders most of the letters dealing with forests; Hugues de la Celle is the expert on the Saintonge-Poitou area; Guillaume de Marcilly and Guillaume Cocatrix have been given the task of buying land and houses to make room for the extension of the royal palace. Others seem to have more general interests; in this group Nogaret, as keeper of the seal, and Marigny, as financial expert, are conspicuous but not unique. They are no busier than some of their colleagues and they have no exclusive powers; for example, Marigny is far from being the only councillor to deal with financial matters. Neither Nogaret nor Marigny is in the position of a chief minister; there is no chain of command which passes through them. They are merely two of a group of fifteen or so men who are very busy writing letters in the king's name. If there is any direction to this activity at all, it must come either from the group as a whole (and it seems a little large to act as a unit), or from the king.

This leads to the most surprising fact of all. Out of a sample of 658 documents taken from registers JJ45 through JJ50, 280 bear the notation "per dominum regem." That is, over two fifths of a very ordinary batch of letters were ordered by the king in person. In many cases there seems to be no very good reason for the king to take a personal interest, and it is impossible to establish categories of letters which were warranted by the king alone. Most pardons, most amortizations, most gifts to churches and royal favorites were ordered by the king, but letters in all of these categories were also warranted by members of the Council. While most acts dealing with the royal family were ordered by the king, this was not always the case. Of a series of marriage contracts involving the Valois branch of the family, three were warranted by the lord of Chambli and Philippe le Convers, one by the keeper of the seal, and only two by the king. Favors for the dowager queen, who was not on good terms with her stepson, were usually ordered by members of the Council. On the other hand, while the king did not always act in cases where he might have been expected to do so, he frequently took responsibility for ratifying farms of the royal domain, exchanges of property between subjects, and marriage contracts of quite ordinary people. These were all routine acts which could have been accomplished by any councillor.

It might be argued that these mentions of the king are purely formal, that he was merely approving acts which had been decided on by others. But if this were true, it would be difficult to explain why the chancery clerks thought there was a difference between letters ordered by the king and those ordered by members of the Council. It would also be difficult to explain why almost all letters warranted "per dominum regem" were written by a single notary, Maillard, and why Maillard seldom prepared letters for anyone else. If Philip's warrant were mere form, any notary could have written the document; only if the king took a personal interest would he need a personal scribe.

Moreover, there is some reason for believing that letters ordered by the keeper of the seal sometimes reflected a personal command by the king. On at least two occasions, Philip sent a personal letter to Nogaret ordering him to prepare letters under the great seal. There is also an interesting case in which two letters ordered by the king were canceled, apparently because they lacked some details, and replaced by fuller letters ordered by the keeper of the seal. Here the keeper probably took the king's letters as warrants for the preparation of his own. Finally, we have a few cases in which the scribe notes that the keeper told him the king had ordered the letter written. Even if only a few of the letters ordered by the keeper of the seal were actually commanded by the king, it would still raise the proportion of letters in which the king took a personal interest to almost fifty per cent of the total.

To sum up, the impression given by this material is that the king controlled and directed the routine work of the government. He was the one who assigned tasks to his councillors, and he reserved the right to act directly and personally in any matter which interested him. There were too many councillors, and responsibility was too evenly divided among them, for any single minister to dominate the government. At the very least, the king was busier than any member of his Council; he was informed about a great variety of matters and he made many decisions. Certainly Philip was not the lazy king who, according to some chroniclers, did nothing but hunt, nor yet the stupid king described by Bernard Saisset who understood nothing and only stared at people.

II

This king who took such interest in the small details of government cannot have been indifferent to greater affairs. If no one councillor was given full responsibility for handling routine business, it is a little difficult to believe that any councillor had unlimited power in making important decisions. We may therefore place more confidence in the scattered notes in the *Olim*, which show the king intervening in cases which came before the *parlement*, making decisions, ordering punishments, suspending sentences, reversing previous acts, directing that inquests be held. We may also believe that the rare references in financial documents to direct intervention by the king[6] would be more numerous if we had fuller records. And we can be reasonably sure that the king who intervenes in both judicial and financial business is Philip the Fair in person and not some vague group of ministers acting in his name.

It seems clear that Philip directed and controlled ordinary operations of government. This raises a strong presumption that he also directed and controlled the government when it made major policy decisions. But presumption is not proof, and it is precisely in this area that Philip seems to be screened most completely by his ministers. His opinions and wishes are never expressed; it is the ministers who make the accusations against Boniface VIII and against the Temple, who draw up the lawsuits which nag the king of England and the count of Flanders into war, who prepare the way for the annexation of Lyons and other imperial territories by adroit diplomacy and propaganda. And it is precisely on

---

[6] Bib[liothèque] Nat[ionale], Ms. lat. 9018, no. 47: a list of difficult points in the accounts of All Saints, 1298; two are marked "must be discussed with the king." An accusation against Betin Caucinel, a master of the royal mints, published by C. V. Langlois in *Revue historique,* LX (1896), 327, suggests that Philip took a personal interest in having accounts carefully checked: " . . . for, concerning one of your simple bailiffs, sire, you want your council to know the truth, so that it can judge him for you, and you want to know whether he submits good and truthful accounts."

such matters that the foreign ambassadors complain that they can never get a personal interview with the king, that Philip will answer only with and through his Council.[7]

And yet, even here there is some evidence to show that the king made the final decisions. The basic policies of the reign appear quite early, long before famous ministers such as Flote or Nogaret or Marigny play any role in the central government. For example. pressure by royal officials on the Church increased sharply in the first years of the reign; by 1291 Nicholas IV could say that the churches of France were complaining daily of grave injuries. Attempts to annex imperial territories were also well under way by the early 1290's. . . .

Moreover, there are a few cases in which we can penetrate the screen of conciliar anonymity and see the king making decisions. One of the best examples is the discussion in the Council following the arrest of Bernard Saisset. There is a long report of the argument between the clerical and the lay members of the Council over the treatment of the bishop; the churchmen naturally wanted to be lenient, while the laymen were angry and urged severe punishment. Philip had to intervene repeatedly, and while the speeches ascribed to him probably do not give his exact words, it is clear that he made the final decisions in a badly divided Council. He was willing to proceed with the case, but he wanted it done with as little scandal as possible — a policy which pleased neither faction.

Thus Philip made the decision which was to lead to the final quarrel with Boniface VIII. We can only speculate about the king's role during the acute stages of the quarrel. The formal approval given in his name to the acts of Nogaret could cover anything from mere acquiescence to active participation. But it has often been pointed out that, once Boniface was dead, Philip could have settled the whole dispute quickly, and on favorable terms, by sacrificing Nogaret. Nogaret himself seems to have feared this, since he begged the king to maintain his cause. Philip accepted the responsibility; only when Nogaret was absolved on easy terms did he make a final settlement. Yet this settlement was reached during a period when Marigny was rising to prominence; it is hard to see why Marigny, or any other leading member of the Council, should have been so anxious to protect a rival. Nogaret certainly believed that he needed the king's support, and it is doubtful that anyone else could have saved him from severe penalties. On the other hand, it is difficult to see why Philip should have been so anxious to protect Nogaret if he felt that Nogaret was entirely responsible for the difficulties which followed Anagni. Only if Philip had made the policy was it his duty to protect a minister who had merely acted as an agent. . . .

III

This long discussion has still not resolved the contradiction with which the paper began. On the one hand, there is too much evidence that Philip took an

---

[7] Heinrich Finke, *Acta Aragonensia* (Berlin, 1908–22), I, 455: Philip refuses to discuss a marriage treaty because "his council was not there"; I, 462: he refuses to speak with envoys of Aragon about the Val d'Aran because "those from his council who ought to take part in this business were not there." It should be noted that in each case Philip had good reasons for wishing to evade an interview. There was little to be gained by a marriage alliance with Aragon, and the French claim to the Val d'Aran was so weak that delay was the best tactic.

active part in both small and great affairs to write him down as a figurehead. On the other hand, it is clear that both individual ministers and the Council as a whole had too much power and responsibility to be dismissed as rubber-stamps. And the king's habit of letting his ministers speak for him on the most important occasions cannot be explained as just a political trick; it seems to have expressed a deep-seated conviction that this was the proper way to act.

The contradiction can be resolved only if we remember a fact which Philip's contemporaries never let him forget: that he was the grandson of St. Louis. He had grown up in a court which was saturated with memories of the holy king; he had worked hard to secure the canonization of his grandfather; it was only natural that he should seek to imitate this model monarch. This meant, first of all, piety, and few historians have ever doubted that Philip was honestly and sincerely pious. But with the piety went a deep sense of the dignity, the greatness, and the mission of French kingship. The king was the high priest of the "religion of monarchy," remote, aloof, withdrawn from all vulgar quarrels. He was to be approached only through his acolytes; the sacred mysteries were not to be revealed to the profane. Finally, a good king did not govern arbitrarily; he did not act on his own whims or make decisions in haste. He must be surrounded by "prud'hommes" who advised and informed him; he must always take counsel before acting. St. Louis had felt that even in the midst of a battle he must hold a council before changing his plans. Philip the Fair acted the same way in the midst of his political battles. But no one has ever doubted that St. Louis made his own decisions after asking for advice, and there is no reason to suppose that Philip

was any more bound by the opinions of his Council.

The best phrase to describe Philip is somewhat anachronistic; he wanted to be a "constitutional" king. But if we give the word "constitutional" its broadest meaning it is a fair description of his policy. Philip tried to conform to the traditions of the French monarchy and the practices of the French government. As far as possible, he governed his realm through a well-established system of courts and administrative officials. He always asked the advice of responsible men; he was influenced by that advice in working out the details of his general policy. He tried to stay at least within the letter of the law; he tried to observe the customs of the kingdom. When he had to go beyond established custom he always sought to justify his action and to obtain the consent of those who were affected. This is why he called the Estates General to hear explanations of his policy toward Boniface VIII and the Templars, why he sought approval of unusual taxes from local assemblies, why, when he annexed the Lyonnais and imposed an onerous treaty on Flanders, he sent his agents to obtain the consent of each community which was affected by his acts. At the very least, consent satisfied the king's desire to remain within the limits of legality. Often, of course, it had important political consequences as well; it certainly facilitated the collection of taxes and strengthened the monarchy in the struggle with Boniface VIII.

If we think of Philip as a "constitutional" king we see why he preferred to work through his ministers and Council. This was the proper and customary way to act; it showed that the king was taking the advice of men learned in precedents and in the law. It preserved the king as a symbol of unity, far above transitory disputes and petty considerations of gain or loss. But it does not mean that Philip refused responsibility and allowed others to govern in his name. He worked hard at his job of being a king; he knew what was going on in his kingdom, and no important act could be accomplished until he made the final decision.

This is not to say that Philip was the model of a wise and just king. His will was stronger than his intelligence; he could be led astray by the very intensity of his belief in the Christian faith and the French monarchy. His piety was as narrow as it was deep; if his own conscience could be satisfied by appropriate forms and phrases, he often failed to realize what consequences his acts might have for others. His faith in the mission of the French monarchy was so broad that it tended to blot out any other considerations—the interests of Western Christendom as a whole, or the rights and welfare of his subjects. He sought moral and legal justification for all his acts, but he was easily persuaded that in any dispute right was entirely on his side and that opposition to his will was inexcusable. His real respect for custom and for law was vitiated by his tendency to accept appearances for reality. If the proper legal forms had been used in a suit to establish royal rights, if a plausible case had been made for the annexation of a border territory, if an assembly had given official support to his policy, he was not apt to inquire too closely how these results had been achieved.

Royal officials knew of these weaknesses and sought to exploit them. Their interest clearly lay in extending royal power, and if they could achieve this end by playing on the king's piety and pride in the French monarchy they naturally did so. Thus the king was told repeatedly that it was his duty as a Christian ruler to persevere in the charges against Boniface VIII and against the Temple. Philip was undoubtedly influenced by this pressure, just as any ruler, no matter how strong, is influenced by the advice of his immediate subordinates. It is even probable that his tactics were altered by the advice that he received. For example, his growing caution in the last years of the reign may reflect Marigny's worries about finance, just as his aggressiveness in the period 1297–1302 may owe something to Flote's impetuous nature. (On the other hand, the young, energetic king may have sought out an aggressive minister, and the tired, middle-aged ruler may have looked for a cautious adviser.) But the fact that ministers may have influenced the king's tactics does not mean that they determined his basic strategy. They all submitted memorandums to him on important questions, and the mere act of submitting memorandums shows that the final decision lay with the king. And the fact that the broad outlines of policy remain consistent from one end of the reign to the other indicates that individual decisions had to be fitted into a general plan which only Philip could have established. No one, not even the king's badly spoiled brother Valois, could make him take much interest in the affairs of Italy. No one, not even the cautious Marigny, could make him give up entirely his attempt to reduce Flanders to obedience. None of his highly placed ecclesiastical advisers could persuade him to quash the charges against Bernard Saisset, or to abandon his policy of restricting the political power of the Church.

In fact, Philip's relations with his Council were not unlike those of a modern prime minister with his cabinet. Special tasks were assigned to each member, advice was always asked and often taken, but final decision and general direction of policy remained with the king. This relationship made it easy for Philip to be a "constitutional" king. He could allow his officials to act in his name because he knew that they would serve his purposes. He could follow due process of law, he could work through official channels, he could always ask for the opinion of his Council because, in the last analysis, he controlled the government. He did not have to set up a group of household officers to control the official government, as his contemporary, Edward I, did; the government was but an extension of his household and he was very much at home in any of its offices. No bureau was autonomous; no minister was strong enough to make his will prevail; no organ of public opinion had any real power. Philip took responsibility for his reign in his own lifetime;[8] he must be allowed to bear that responsibility in the judgment of historians.

---

[8] On his deathbed Philip is reported to have said that he had received bad advice but that "he himself was the cause of his bad advice." C. Baudon de Mony, "La mort et les funerailles de Philippe le Bel," *Bibliothèque de l'École des Chartes,* LVIII (1897), 12.

MANDELL CREIGHTON (1843–1901) was bishop
of London and first editor of the *English Historical
Review*. He wrote widely on the history of the
Middle Ages and on the age of Elizabeth. When his
*History of the Papacy from the Great Schism to the
Sack of Rome* began to appear in 1882, it was quickly
accepted as a classic account of the papacy during
the Renaissance. In the first chapter of this work
Creighton gives his assessment of the pontificate of
Boniface VIII and of its significance in papal history.*

Mandell Creighton

Halfway House from
Gregory VII to Luther

The change that passed over Europe
in the sixteenth century was due to the
development of new conceptions, political, intellectual, and religious, which
found their expression in a period of
bitter conflict. The state-system of Europe was remodelled, and the mediaeval
ideal of a united Christendom was replaced by a struggle of warring nation-
alities. The Papal monarchy over the
Western Church was attacked and over-
thrown. The traditional basis of the ecclesiastical system was impugned, and in
some countries rejected, in favour of the
authority of Scripture. The study of
classical antiquity engendered new forms
of thought, and created an enquiring

criticism which gave a new tendency to
the mental activity of Europe.

The processes by which these results
were achieved were not isolated, but influenced one another. However important each may be in itself, it cannot be
profitably studied when considered apart
from the reaction of the rest. The object
of the following pages is to trace, within
a limited sphere, the working of the
causes which brought about the change
from mediaeval to modern times. The
history of the Papacy affords the widest
field for such an investigation; for the
Papacy was a chief element in the political system, and was supreme over the
ecclesiastical system of the Middle Ages,

*From Mandell Creighton, *A History of the Papacy from the Great Schism to the Sack of Rome* (London: Longmans, Green, and Co., 1897), vol. 1, pp. 3–5, 7–8, 13, 14–16, 18, 21, 24–25, 27–32.

while round it gathered much that was most characteristic of the changing intellectual life of Europe.

The period which we propose to traverse may be defined as that of the decline of the Papal monarchy over Western Europe. The abasement of the Papacy by the Great Schism of the fourteenth century intensified Papal aggressions and wrought havoc in the organisation of the Church. The schemes of reform which consequently agitated Christendom showed a widespread desire for change. Some of these movements were held to pass beyond reform to revolution, and were consequently suppressed, while the plans of the conservative reformers failed through national jealousies and want of statesmanship. After the failure of these attempts at organic reform the chief European kingdoms redressed their most crying grievances by separate legislation or by agreements with the Pope. A reaction, that was skilfully used, restored the Papacy to much of its old supremacy; but, instead of profiting by the lessons of adversity, the Papacy only sought to minimise or abolish the concessions which had been wrung from its weakness. Impelled by the growing feeling of nationality, it sought a firm basis for itself as a political power in Italy, whereby it regained prestige in Europe, and identified itself with the Italian mind at its most fertile epoch. But by its close identification with Italy, the Papacy, both in national and intellectual matters, drifted apart from Germany; and the result was a Teutonic and national rebellion against the Papal monarchy—a rebellion so far successful that it divided Europe into two opposing camps, and brought to light differences of national character, of political aim and intellectual ideas, which had grown up unnoticed till conflict forced them into conscious expression.

Important as this period may be, it deals only with one or two phases of the history of the Papacy. Before we trace the steps in the decline of the Papal monarchy, it will be useful to recall briefly the means by which it rose and the way in which it was interwoven with the state-system of Europe.

The history of the early Church shows that even in Apostolic times the Christian congregations felt a need of organisation. Deacons were chosen by popular election to provide for the due ministration of Christian benevolence, and elders were appointed to be rulers and instructors of the congregation. As the Apostles passed away, the need of presidency over meetings of the representatives of congregations developed the order of bishops, and led to the formation of districts within which their authority was exercised. The political life which had been extinguished under the Roman Imperial system began to revive in the organisation of the Church, and the old feeling of civic government found in the regulation of ecclesiastical affairs a new field for its exercise. A line of separation was gradually drawn between the clergy and the laity, and the settlement of controversies concerning the Christian faith gave ample scope for the activity of the clerical order. Frequent assemblies were held for the discussion of disputed points, and the pre-eminence of the bishops of the chief cities was gradually established over other bishops. The clergy claimed authority over the laity; the control of the bishop over the inferior clergy grew more definite; and the bishop in turn recognised the superiority of his metropolitan. In the third century the Christian Churches formed a powerful and active confederacy with an organised and graduated body of officials. . . .

The precedence of the Bishop of Rome

over other bishops was a natural growth of the conditions of the times. The need of organisation was forced upon the Church by internal discords and the hardships of stormy days: the traditions of organisation were a bequest from the Imperial system. . . .

The fall of the shadowy Empire of the West, and the union of the Imperial power in the person of the ruler of Constantinople, brought a fresh accession of dignity and importance to the Bishop of Rome. The distant Emperor could exercise no real power over the West. The Ostrogothic kingdom in Italy scarcely lasted beyond the life-time of its great founder, Theodoric. The wars of Justinian only served to show how scanty were the benefits of the Imperial rule. The invasion of the Lombards united all dwellers in Italy in an endeavour to escape the lot of servitude and save their land from barbarism. In this crisis it was found that the Imperial system had crumbled away, and that the Church alone possessed a strong organisation. In the decay of the old municipal aristocracy the people of the towns gathered round their bishops, whose sacred character inspired some respect in the barbarians, and whose active charity lightened the calamities of their flocks. . . .

It was [in the latter half of the ninth century] that the Papacy first stood forward as the centre of the state-system of Europe. The [Carolingian] Empire had fallen after having given an expression, as emphatic as it was brief, to the political ideas that lay deep in the minds of men. The unity embodied in the Empire of Charles [Charlemagne] had been broken up into separate states; but it still was possible to combine these states into a theocracy under the rule of the Pope. The theory of the Papal monarchy over the Church was not the result merely of grasping ambition and intrigue on the part of individual Popes; it corresponded rather to the deep-seated belief of Western Christendom. . . . If the decay of the Frankish monarchy had not involved the destruction of order throughout Europe, the Papacy might have won its way rapidly to supreme temporal as well as spiritual power. But the end of the ninth century was a time of wild confusion. Saracens, Normans, Slavs plundered and conquered almost at will, and the Frankish kings and the Popes were equally powerless to maintain their position. The great vassals among the Franks destroyed the power of the monarchy. The fall of the Imperial power in Italy deprived the Popes of their protector, and left them helpless instruments in the hands of the Italian nobles, who were called their vassals. . . .

From this common abasement the temporal power was the first to rise. The German peoples within the Empire of Charles the Great were at length united by the urgent necessity of protecting themselves against barbarous foes. They formed a strong elective monarchy, and shook themselves loose from their Romanised brethren, the Western Franks, amongst whom the power of the vassals was still to maintain disunion for centuries. The German kingdom was the inheritor of the ideas and policy of Charles the Great, and the restoration of the Imperial power was a natural and worthy object of the Saxon line of kings. The restoration of the Empire involved a restoration also of the Papacy. But this was not left solely to political considerations. A revival of Christian feeling found a centre in the great monastery of Cluny, and the monastic reformers . . . aimed at uniting Christendom under the headship of the Pope. Their immediate objects were to bring back the clergy to purer and more spiritual lives, and to check the secularisation of the clerical office which the growing wealth of the Church and the lax discipline of stormy times had gradually wrought. Their cry was for the strict enforcement of the celibacy of the clergy and the suppression of simony. They felt, however, that reform must begin with the head, and that no one could restore the Papacy except the Emperor. Henry III was hailed as a second David, when at the Synod of Sutri [1046] he superintended the deposition of three simoniacal or profligate Popes who were struggling for the chair of S. Peter. Then under a noble line of German popes the Papacy was again identified with the highest spiritual life of Christendom, and learned to borrow the strength of the Imperial system, under whose shadow it grew to power.

This condition of tutelage to the Empire could not long continue. . . . So soon as the Papacy was re-established it aimed at independence. The next objects of the reformers were to make Rome the centre of the new ideas, to secure for the Papacy a safe position in Rome itself, and to free it from its dependence on the Empire. Their leading spirit was an Italian monk, Hildebrand of Saona, who, both at Rome and Cluny, had studied the reforming policy, and then, with keen and sober appreciation of the task that lay before him, set himself to give it effect. . . .

When at length the time was ripe, Hildebrand ascended the Papal throne as Gregory VII. Full of zeal and enthusiasm, he was desirous of carrying out the grandest schemes. . . . In ecclesiastical matters Gregory enunciated the infallibility of the Pope, his power of deposing bishops and restoring them at his own will, the necessity of his consent to give universal validity to synodal decrees, his

supreme and irresponsible jurisdiction, the precedence of his legates over all bishops. In political matters he asserted that the name of Pope was incomparable with any other, that he alone could use the insignia of empire, that he could depose emperors, that all princes ought to kiss his feet, that the could relase from their allegiance the subjects of wicked rulers. Such were the magnificent claims which Gregory VII bequeathed to the mediaeval Papacy, and pointed out the way towards their realisation.

Such views as these necessarily led to a struggle between the temporal and spiritual power. The conflict was first with the Empire, which was connected in the most vital way with the Papacy. Gregory VII was happy in his adversary, the profligate and careless Henry IV. Strong as were the opponents whom the rigorous policy of Gregory raised up, the opponents of the misgovernment of Henry were still stronger. The Saxons rose in revolt against a ruler of the house of Franconia; the enemies of the King combined with the Pope, and Henry's moral weakness gave Gregory the opportunity of impressing by a striking dramatic act his view of the Papal power upon the imagination of Europe. Three days did the humbled monarch in the courtyard of the castle of Canossa sue for absolution from the triumphant Pope [1077]. . . . The humilation of Henry IV was made a type to posterity of the relations between the temporal and spiritual power. . . .

It was reserved, however, for Innocent III [1198–1216] to realise most fully the ideas of Hildebrand. If Hildebrand was the Julius, Innocent was the Augustus, of the Papal Empire. He had not the creative genius nor the fiery energy of his great forerunner; but his clear intellect never missed an opportunity, and his calculating spirit rarely erred from its mark. A man of severe and lofty character, which inspired universal respect, he possessed all the qualities of an astute political intriguer. He was lucky in his opportunities, as he had no formidable antagonist; among the rulers of Europe his was the master mind. In every land he made the Papal power decisively felt. In Germany, France, and England, he dictated the conduct of the Kings. . . . The change which he wrought in the attitude of the Papacy may be judged from the fact that, whereas his predecessors had contented themselves with the title of Vicar of Peter, Innocent assumed the name of Vicar of Christ. Europe was to form a great theocracy under the direction of the Pope.

If Innocent III thus realised the Hildebrandine ideal of the Papacy, he at the same time opened up a dangerous field for its immediate activity. Innocent III may be called the founder of the States of the Church. . . Innocent III was the first Pope who claimed and exercised the rights of an Italian prince. . . . He obtained from the Emperor Otto IV (1201) the cession of all the lands which the Papacy claimed, and so established for the first time an undisputed title to the Papal States. Innocent was an Italian as well as a Churchman. As a Churchman he wished to bring all the kings and princes of Europe into submission to the Papal power; as an Italian he aimed at freeing Italy from foreign rulers, and uniting it into one State under the Papal sway.

In this new sphere which Innocent opened up lay the great danger of Innocent's successors. The Papal monarchy over the Church had won its way to universal recognition, and the claim of the Papacy to interfere in the internal affairs of European States had been established. It was natural for the Papacy at the height of its power to strive after a firm territorial basis on which to rest secure; what had been gained by moral superiority must be kept by political force. However distant nations might tremble before the Papal decrees, it often happened that the Pope himself was exiled from his capital by the turbulent rabble of the city, or was fleeing before foes whom his Imperial antagonist could raise against him at his very gates. The Papacy was only obeying a natural instinct of self-preservation in aiming at a temporal sovereignty which would secure it against temporal mishaps.

Yet the whole significance of the Papacy was altered when this desire to secure a temporal sovereignty in Italy became a leading feature of the Papal policy. The Papacy still held the same position in the eyes of men, and its existence was still held necessary to maintain the fabric of Christendom; but a Pope straining every nerve to defend his Italian possessions did not appeal to men's sympathies. So long as the Papacy had been fighting for ecclesiastical privileges, or for the establishment of its own dignity and importance, it had been fighting for an idea which in the days of feudal oppression awakened as much enthusiasm as does a struggle for freedom in our own day. When the Papacy entered into a war to extend its own possessions, it might win glorious victories, but they were won at a ruinous cost. . . .

Immersed in narrow schemes of self-interest, the Popes lost their real strength in the respect and sympathies of Europe. Instead of being the upholders of ecclesiastical independence, they became the oppressors of the clergy and the infringers of ecclesiastical rights. Hence, in France, lawyers developed a fruitful conception of the liberties of the Gallican Church—freedom of patrons from Papal interference, freedom of election to chapters, and a prohibition of Papal taxation except with the consent of the Church and the Crown. Instead of being the upholders of civil liberty, the Popes ranked with the princes of Europe and had no sympathy with the cause of the people. . . .

In this career of purely political enterprise the Papacy again became associated with the factions of contending families in Rome, till in 1292 the assembled Cardinals were so equally divided between the parties that they found it impossible to elect. At last, in utter weariness, they chose a holy hermit of the Abruzzi, Piero da Morrone, whose fame for piety was in the mouths of men. The Pontificate of Celestine V, for such was the name Morrone assumed, might seem to be a caricature on the existing state of the Papacy. A man had been elected Pope by a sudden impulse solely for his holiness: no sooner was he elected than the Cardinals felt that holiness was not the quality most requisite for the high office of Head of the Church. Never did election awaken more enthusiasm among the people, yet never was Pope more powerless for good. Ignorant of politics, of business, of the ways of the world, Celestine V became a helpless instrument in the hands of the King of Naples. He gave up the government of the Church to others, and bestowed his favours with reckless prodigality. The crowd thronged around him whenever he went abroad to crave his blessing; a new order, the Celestinians, was founded by those who were eager to model their life on his; but the Cardinals groaned in secret dismay over the perils with which his incompetence

threatened the Papacy. After a pontificate of five months he abdicated, to the joy of the Cardinals, and to the grief of the people, which showed itself in hatred for his successor. Henceforth it was clear that the Papacy had become a great political institution: its spiritual significance had been merged in its worldly importance. It needed a statesman to baffle princes by his astuteness, not a saint to kindle by his holiness spiritual aspirations among the masses.

Celestine's successor, Boniface VIII, attempted, when it was too late, to launch the Papacy upon a new career. Though endowed with all the fire of Gregory VII, and with the keen political instincts of Innocent IV, he failed to understand either the disastrous results to the Papacy of the policy of his predecessors, or the hidden strength of the opposition which it had kindled. The Papacy had destroyed the Empire, but in its victory had fallen with its foe. In overthrowing the Empire it had weakened the outward expression of the idea on which its own power was founded, and had first used, and then betrayed, the growing feeling of nationality, which was the rising enemy of the mediaeval system. When Boniface VIII aimed at absorbing into the Papacy the Imperial power, when he strove to weld together Europe into a great confederacy, over which the Pope was to preside, at once the head of its religion and the administrator of a system of international law, he only brought to light the gulf which had been slowly widening between the aims of the Papacy and the aspirations of Europe. His weapons were the weapons of this world, and though his utterances might assume the cover of religious phrases, his arts were those of an adventurous politician. First he resolved to secure himself in Rome, which he did by the remorseless overthrow of the Colonna family. In the rest of Italy he aimed at bringing about order by crushing the Ghibellins and putting the Guelfs in power. . . .

While these were his measures in Italy, Boniface VIII advanced with no less boldness and decision elsewhere. He demanded that the Kings of England and France should submit their differences to his arbitration. When they refused he tried to make war impossible without his consent by cutting off one great source of supplies, and issued a bull, forbidding the taxation of the clergy, except by the consent of the Pope. But in England Boniface was repelled by the vigorous measures of Edward I, who taught the clergy that, if they would not contribute to the maintenance of civil government, they should not have the advantages of its protection. In France, Philip IV retaliated by forbidding the export of gold or silver from his realm without the royal consent. Boniface was thus cut off from the supplies which the Papacy raised for itself by taxation of the clergy. Even while professing to fight the battle of clerical privilege, Boniface could not carry with him the staunch support of the clergy themselves. They had experienced the fiscal oppression of Pope and King equally, and found that the Pope was the more intolerable of the two. If they had to submit to the tender mercies of one or the other, the King was at least more amenable to reason. For a time Boniface had to give way; but circumstances soon seemed to favour him. . . .

Yet Boniface could not read the signs of the times. He was misled by the outburst of popular enthusiasm and religious zeal which followed the establishment of a year of jubilee in 1300. The crusading age was past and gone; but the spirit that animated the Crusades still survived in Europe. The restless desire to visit a holy place and see with their bodily eyes some guarantee of the reality of their devotion, drove crowds of pilgrims to Rome to earn by prayers and offerings the promised absolution for their sins. Others since the days of Boniface have been misled as to the real strength of a system, by taking as their measure the outbursts of feverish enthusiasm which it could at times call forth. Men trampled one another to death in their eagerness to reach the tombs of the Apostles; yet in three short years the Vicar of S. Peter found no one to rescue him from insult and outrage.

The breach between Boniface VIII and Philip IV went on widening. As the Pope grew more resolute in asserting his pretensions, the King gathered the French clergy and people more closely around him. The growth of legal studies had raised up a class of lawyers who could meet the Pope on his own ground. As he fortified himself by the principles of the canon law, the French legists rested on the principles of the old civil law of Rome. The canon law, in setting up the Pope as supreme over the Church, had but followed the example of the civil law, which traced its own origin to the Imperial pleasure. The two systems now met in collision, and their fundamental identity rendered compromise impossible. Angry bulls and letters followed one another. The Pope furbished up all the weapons in his armoury. On doctrinal grounds he asserted that, "as God made two lights, the greater light to rule the day, and the lesser light to rule the night," so He set up two jurisdictions, the temporal and the spiritual, of which the spiritual is greater, and involves the temporal in point of right, though not necessarily in point of use. On historical grounds he asserted: "Our predecessors have deposed three Kings of France, and if any King did the wrong which they did, we would depose him like a servant." Against this was set up the intelligible principle, that in things temporal the King held his power subject to God alone. Both sides prepared for extremities. Philip's lawyers accused the Pope of heresy, of crime, of simony, and appealed to a General Council of the Church. Boniface excommunicated Philip, and prepared to pronounce against him the sentence of dethronement, releasing his subjects from their allegiance. But Philip's plans were cunningly laid, and he had Italian craft to help him. The day before the bull of deposition was to have been published, Boniface was made prisoner by a band of Philip's adherents. The exiled Italian, Sciarra Colonna, planned the attack, and the acuteness of the Tolosan, Guillaume de Nogaret, one of Philip's lawyers, helped to make its success complete. As he sat, unsuspecting of evil, in the retirement of his native Anagni, Boniface was suddenly surprised and maltreated, without a blow being struck in his behalf. It is true that on the third day of his captivity he was rescued; but his prestige was gone. Frenzied, or heartbroken, we know not which, he died a month after his release.

With Boniface VIII fell the mediaeval Papacy. He had striven to develop the idea of the Papal monarchy into a definite system. He had claimed for it the noble position of arbiter amongst the nations of Europe. Had he succeeded, the power which, according to the mediaeval theory of Christendom, was vested in the Empire, would have passed over to the Papacy no longer as a theoretical right, but as an actual possession; and the Papacy would have asserted its supremacy over the rising state-system of Europe. His failure showed that with the destruction of the Empire the Papacy had fallen likewise. Both continued to exist in name, and set forth their old pretensions; but the Empire, in its old aspect of head of Christendom, had become a name of the past or a dream of the future since the failure of Frederick II. The failure of Boniface VIII showed that a like fate had overtaken the Papacy likewise. The suddenness and abruptness of the calamity which befell Boniface impressed this indelibly on the minds of men. The Papacy had first shown its power by a great dramatic act; its decline was manifested in the same way. The drama of Anagni is to be set against the drama of Canossa.

F. M. POWICKE (1879–1963) has frequently been
called one of the outstanding English medievalists of
the twentieth century. While the bulk of his mature
work, notably *King Henry III and the Lord Edward*
and *The Thirteenth Century 1216–1307,* was concerned
with England, the range of his knowledge and interests
was in fact much wider. He approached each problem
he faced with a grasp both of its detail and of the total
background of medieval development against which,
he insisted, that problem was to be viewed and
understood. In 1932, the fiftieth anniversary of the
publication of Creighton's book, he took the
opportunity to assess it and to offer his own opinion
on the significance of Boniface VIII. His interpretation
should be compared not only with Creighton's but also
with Flick's, the opening selection in the present book.*

F. M. Powicke

The Culmination of Medieval Papalism

Bishop Creighton entitled his book
*A History of the Papacy from the Great
Schism to the Sack of Rome.* He prefixed
two introductory chapters, the one on
the rise of the papal power, the other
on the popes at Avignon. As he read its
history, the papacy dominated Europe
for rather more than two centuries. Pope
Gregory VII revealed it, in all its strength,
after a long period of preparation. Pope
Boniface VIII, in spite of his high asser-
tion of its pretensions, disclosed its weakness. "The suddenness and abruptness
of the calamity which befell Boniface
impressed" the fate of the papal power
"indelibly on the minds of men. The
papacy had first shown its power by a
great dramatic act; its decline was manifested in the same way. The drama of

Anagni is to be set against the drama of
Canossa." The disgraceful captivity of
later popes in Avignon, the still more
disgraceful schism, the efforts of the
Church in the Conciliar movement to
find a way to a corporate reconstruction,
the re-establishment of an Italian papacy
which maintained its local power by a
system of concordats with European
princes, finally the Reformation and the
division of Italy into spheres of interest
between great Catholic powers, followed
naturally, if not inevitably, from the
collapse revealed to the world on the mor-
row of the great jubilee of the year 1300.
The drama of Anagni in 1303 stands halfway in history between the humiliation
of the emperor Henry IV by Pope Gregory VII and the sack of Rome by the

*From F. M. Powicke, *The Christian Life in the Middle Ages* (Oxford, 1935), pp. 48–73. Reprinted by
permission of the Clarendon Press, Oxford. Footnotes omitted.

soldiers of the emperor Charles V. It divides, both in time and in the logic of human affairs, the story of the later, the real, Middle Ages.

Fifty years have gone by since Creighton, in 1882, published the first two volumes of his history from his college living in Northumberland . . . and this particular half-century has seen more intense activity spent upon the problems of medieval history, notably, perhaps, in the age of Dante and Boniface VIII, than in all previous centuries. Does Creighton's judgement still stand? The answer is Yes and No. That the last years of the thirteenth century, when the Crusades came to an end, and French and Spanish powers were established in the Mediterranean, were a turning-point in European history, is realized now better than it has ever been realized before. That papal power in the fourteenth century was a different thing from the power of Gregory VII or Innocent III is a commonplace of accepted history. At the same time, our conception of the process of transition from one stage of history to the other has been greatly enriched. The emphasis is different from that suggested by the clear-cut generalizations and the dramatic moments upon which historians insisted fifty years ago. Conventional judgements, if they do not ring false, fall like thin and twittering cries upon the ear, as the crowded scenes, the incessant variety of purpose, opinion and passion, amidst which Pope Boniface had to make himself felt, are revealed to us. And the Pope himself falls into place, as he ceases to move before us like a buskined figure of tragedy and becomes a man. . . . I am [here] concerned with some aspects of this rich variety, rather than with the ghostly refinements of reflection which we call the verdict of history.

Few episodes in medieval history are better known than the brief pontificate of Pope Celestine V in the year 1294. After violent quarrels at Rome, the Sacred College, by this time reduced to an oligarchy of eleven cardinals, had gathered together, in October 1293, at Perugia. The cardinals sat in conclave for nine months, unable to agree. . . . At last, partly from weariness, partly through the more informal and secretive manipulations of King Charles [of Naples], the electors were reduced to a mood susceptible to inspiration. The old cardinal of Ostia had been much impressed by the visions of coming disaster seen in this disgraceful period of delay by a holy hermit. Why not end the disgrace and all disputes by the election of the hermit? A common enthusiasm united the college: some had long been affected by the spiritual movements then so widespread in Italy, others were tired of the fierce family ambitions and the political considerations which divided them. So, early in July 1294, Peter of Murrone was elected. . . .

Had Peter of Murrone been merely an obscure solitary, his elevation and retirement would have been but a curious incident in papal history. But he was much more than this. Thirty years before, this uncouth but ardent plebeian had founded an order, known after his pontificate as the Celestine, whose houses were scattered about central and southern Italy; and although he had divested himself, like St. Francis, of all authority over his order and had gone back to his cave on Mount Murrone, he was revered both as its founder and as a saintly man endowed with the gift of prophecy. His election raised the highest hopes in circles far beyond his order. It was welcomed as the fulfilment of the dreams of Joachim of Fiore and St. Francis. The Spiritual Franciscans, whose anxieties were voiced by their poet, Jacopone da Todi, waited in breathless expectation. Would he hold his own? Would he, remote from all party and faction, be the father of all as he had been the father of his brethren? Would he be strong enough to realize on the throne of St. Peter the visions which had come to him in his quiet cell? When he recognized the right of the scattered and persecuted little groups which claimed to be the true Franciscans to live as they willed or to join themselves to his own order, they saw the dawn of the new age. Then came the bewilderment, the bitterness, of the great refusal, soon to be followed by passionate concern for the fate of the master. For Celestine had not been allowed to go back to his own people. His existence was embarrassing enough to the new pope; as the centre, however unwilling, of a fanatical party, and the gathering point of every hostile element, he might be a public danger. He was brought northwards. He eluded his companions and tried to escape. He was found and brought to a cell, like his old cell in Abruzzi, in the castle of Fumone, near the papal city of Anagni. There, in May 1296, he died. Pope Boniface was to find that he was more dangerous dead than alive. Celestine pursued him through the troubles of his reign and tormented his memory after he had joined him in death. Celestine, the story ran, had been harried by his ambitious rival into retirement. The resignation, the work of fraud, was invalid, and Boniface was no true pope. And later, so the legend grew, Celestine had not died a natural death. The new pope had driven a nail into his head. Even his canonization by Pope Clement V ten years after the death of Boniface was a move in the vendetta against the memory of Boniface carried on by his implacable enemies. The political and per-

sonal enemies of Boniface joined mystics and enthusiasts in exalting the one pope and defaming the other. . . .

The contrast between the two popes has been the theme of disputants and historians from their time to this. Any serious estimate of Boniface and his pontificate must, indeed, be an elaboration of this theme. . . .

"Henceforth," wrote Creighton, "it was clear that the papacy had become a great political institution: its spiritual significance had been merged in its worldly importance. It needed a statesman to baffle princes by his astuteness, not a saint to kindle by his holiness spiritual aspirations among the masses." Like most clear-cut judgements, the words give only half the truth. They set aside the "spiritual significance" of the papal system which Boniface accepted as a matter of course; they neglect the practical difficulties which no pope, however great a saint he might be, could hope to escape. For during the thirteenth century the Church, as it surmounted one crisis after another, heard the voice of

> a subtler Sphinx renew
> Riddles of death Thebes never knew.

At one time the Church, in the uneasy impulse to realize its own ideals, had found relief in the movements of monastic reformation. But for rude peoples gradually finding their way in the troublesome, if self-imposed, task of civilization, these were an uncertain means of inspiration. The great process of discipline which culminated in the days of Pope Gregory VII . . . absorbed and directed the monastic revivals, and strove after an independent episcopate, looking to Rome for guidance, a celibate clergy, a common body of law, a clear-cut yet adaptable penitential system, sound and coherent teaching about the sacraments, above all about the Mass, in which the Church daily renewed its life. In the eyes of the great saints, thinkers, and administrators who, during the next two centuries, enriched the Church, the body of doctrine and practice which developed was an organic whole. . . . They did not regard the articulated system of government, however defective, as separable from the deposit of thought and experience, however inscrutable. In our judgement upon any vigorous pope we can never afford to forget the weight and momentum of this great heritage which it was his duty to safeguard. Nor can we impute to his critics or enemies the wisdom of the onlooker or the detachment of the sceptic. He was bound as a President of the United States is bound by the Constitution or an English Prime Minister by the traditions of parliamentary government. Pope Boniface VIII may have been unwise in his choice of the occasion of his great pronouncements, and in the uncompromising vigour of their phrasing, but he was no revolutionary seeking after an unfamiliar world. The famous bull *Unam Sanctam* is one of the most carefully drafted documents which have ever emerged from the papal chancery. It is a formal exposition of the plenitude of papal power, spiritual and temporal, and was later included in the *Extravagantes communes,* a collection of decretals made at the end of the fifteenth century, which became part of the *Corpus Juris Canonici.*[1] In its emphasis upon the derivative nature of secular power—that, while part of the divine order, this has a dependent, not an independent authority—it follows the argument of Giles of Rome, the foremost apologist of the papacy. Two of its main theses are derived, through Giles

---

[1] The official codification of Canon Law.—*Ed.*

and other writers, from a famous passage in Hugh of St. Victor and the equally famous, though much discussed, treatment by St. Bernard of the doctrine of the two swords. In the same year, 1302, in which the bull was issued, the same high claims were admitted in formal terms by the chancellor of Albert of Austria, the emperor-elect.

Anti-papal propaganda, especially in France, had provoked Boniface. But drastic doctrine in politics has often, perhaps always, been made possible by opposition. The doctrines of parliamentary sovereignty and of the divine right of kings were forged from pliable materials in the heat of controversy. The point is that in the eyes of the papalists who looked over Europe about the year 1300, the position of *Unam Sanctam,* if the precious heritage from the past was to be maintained, was the only position to take, and, if logic was to be the order of the day, had its rational and natural roots in the experience of the Church. . . .

The view that the secular is subject to the spiritual power had hardened during the half-century which separated Boniface VIII from the great pope Innocent IV, the first pope to give unequivocal expression to it. Hitherto the prevalent doctrine had been that of the harmonious co-operation, each in its own sphere, of the two powers. As the classic exposition of it by Dante shows, the doctrine of harmony was by no means dead. It was to have importance in later history. But the implacable quarrel between the papacy and the Hohenstaufen emperors had forced the issue of sovereignty. Of two irreconcilable powers, one must be the greater, the sovereign. Pope Boniface took the same view in the face of states which, as they became more firmly knit, more conscious of their unity and of their past, maintained a doctrine of sovereignty of their own. Both Philip the Fair of France and Edward I of England were ready, if pressed, to claim the right of their kingdoms to control their own destinies and to define the secular duties of their own clergy. The king of France, protector of the Church, had, it was argued, no temporal superior. . . .

The cause alike of this entrenchment and of the criticism which it provoked, is to be found in the Crusades. The attempt to explain the Crusades as a social or economic development has lost something of its charm, but we are still inclined, I think, to try to explain them away as an abnormal development in medieval life, and to suppose that Europe had returned to sanity by the time of Pope Boniface. I believe on the contrary that the Holy War . . . was regarded as the function, if not the main duty, of a united Christendom, and that as a mental habit it long survived its practical importance. It was an acknowledgement of the right to use force in behalf of the service of Christ if persuasion and spiritual weapons either failed or were out of place. This teaching began to creep into the law books of the Church in the eleventh century, as part of the Hildebrandine system, and it was supported, if not actually suggested, by extracts from the writings of St. Augustine. It was accepted by earnest men and idealists of all kinds, cut across all divisions of opinion, and, in the days of Pope Boniface, was a common starting-point in minds which seemed to agree about nothing else. . . .

In fact, as was inevitable, the Crusade . . . got in the way of itself. Four great councils of the Church were summoned between 1215 and 1311. At all of them the programme was the pacification of Europe and legislation about outstanding questions in doctrine, discipline, reform

and politics, with a view to united action in the Holy War. . . . The popes appeared as the arbiters of Europe. They assumed the responsibility for creating order and had the disposal of the crusading taxes. On this foundation the material power of the papacy in the thirteenth century was built. By canon law, generally accepted by secular rulers, the taxation of the clergy for temporal purposes was forbidden. With the acquiescence of Christendom the taxation of the clergy by the papacy for spiritual purposes, the defence and advancement of the Church, became an established fact. The application of these revenues, in the name of order and orthodoxy, to further papal policy was the natural, and not illogical, result. That the Crusade was postponed by political difficulties was indisputable. That heresy, schism, and the self-seeking aggrandizement of princes should be put down with the aid of force and of the new papal resources was an easy deduction. The Vicar of Christ could alone decide whether the circumstances justified such action. Hence came the development of papal despotism, and the extension in all directions of the conception of the Holy War; the blurring of the distinction between heresy and opposition to the will of the Pope; the increasing resort to papal taxation and the insistence upon the immunity of the clergy from the taxation of princes, which lie behind the bull *Clericis laicos* and the first quarrel between Boniface and the kings of France and England. Hence the resistance of communities, conscious of their own unity and faced by their own complicated obligations, to a papacy whose intervention with their affairs and their wealth far transcended the activities of Gregory VII or even of Innocent III. And hence the indignation of those who, feeling that everything was wrong in a world so alien from the spirit of St. Francis, spent themselves in prophetic passion.

Such was the heritage of Pope Boniface. He entered upon it with alacrity. When he was elected at the end of 1294 he was over sixty years of age, but he was confident, vigorous and ambitious. . . . That he had encouraged Celestine to resign is more than likely. He can have felt no doubts on the wisdom of that step, just as he had no hesitation in quashing the hasty and ill-advised bulls issued during Celestine's pontificate. Everywhere about him, as he surveyed the political debris left by his predecessors, he saw work waiting to be done. Four years earlier the last Christian stronghold in Syria had fallen. The Holy Land, lying between the Sultanate of Egypt and the Mongolian conquerors of Persia and Mesopotamia, might yet be rescued if the still powerful schismatic churches in the East, the Jacobite and the Nestorian, could be strengthened in their task of converting the Mongols by the intervention of Rome. The affairs of Germany, of Hungary, of Poland demanded attention. Within the ecclesiastical system, many problems, such as the ever-present problem of the relations between the secular and regular clergy, called for decision. But above all, the Sicilian question—the legacy of the Holy War against the Emperor Frederick II and his family—must first be settled. We can see now that the question of Sicily was the beginning of modern political history. Frederick had succeeded the Normans as king of Sicily and South Italy. As emperor, he was unwilling to play the profitable Norman role of vassal and defender of the Holy See. In the course of a fierce crusade he had held his own, but after his death his family had been worn down and destroyed. The French prince, Charles of Anjou, had

been called in, subvented partly by the proceeds of crusading taxes, partly by Florentine bankers; but before Charles died the island of Sicily had revolted and had called in the house of Aragon, which had in its service the greatest sailors of the age. So began the long struggle for the control of the Western Mediterranean. The outcome was the partition of Italy and the rivalries which alined the powers of Europe from the days of Ferdinand and Isabella to the days of Napoleon. But the popes of the later thirteenth century saw in the Sicilian question a rebellious island, the centre of an unrest threatening the peace of Europe and the stability of the Holy See in Italy.[2] When Boniface VIII became pope he found a state of chaos, but he saw his way to a solution. . . . The Pope declared a new Holy War against the traitors. During nearly the whole of his reign this war wasted his resources and the resources of Europe. He had to pay for it. . . . Italy, in papal tenths [tithes], provided 400,000 florins. France 173,000, and England no less than 450,000. This was the background to the dispute about clerical taxation. If, Boniface argued, the clergy of France and England were burdened with the expense of this sacred cause, their canonical protection against the demands of kings must be safeguarded. If, the Kings argued, the clergy can export its wealth to aid the wars of the Pope, it may well be expected to aid us in our and their own wars. The subtle Sphinx had renewed an old riddle.

The Sicilian Crusade was, as I have

---

[2] After the death of Frederick II the pope had ceded Sicily, a papal fief, to Charles of Anjou, a brother of St. Louis. The Sicilian Vespers (1282) had thrown Charles off the island and against papal wishes had led to *de facto* rule in Sicily by the royal house of Aragon. The papacy had never ceased fighting this usurpation and was intermittently aided by France.—*Ed.*

said, the legacy of the struggle with Frederick II and the Hohenstaufen. The viper brood was by no means dead. . . . The Crusade stirred old passions among the Ghibellines of Italy. To what extent the terrible *vendetta* between Boniface and the family of the Colonnas was due to [this cause] . . . is uncertain; but the relations between the Colonna and the man whom Boniface regarded as a schismatic and a traitor [Frederick of Sicily] certainly fed the anger of the Pope, and added to his difficulties. This powerful family turned against Boniface. The two cardinals of Colonna, who had voted for his election, took the lead in the local resistance to him, and, combining with Jacopone da Todi, the Franciscan poet, denied the validity of his election. They and their neighbours in the Campagna had other good grounds for resentment. Boniface from the first made it perfectly clear that he meant to be master in the Papal States and to rely for aid upon his family. . . . As the policy of Boniface became clear, the anti-papal party formed, members of the house of Colonna at its head. One of them, Stephen, a vigorous and cultivated layman, who lived to sound the praises of Petrarch and lives still in Petrarch's letters, seized the treasure of the Pope as it was being conveyed from Anagni to Rome. This exploit was hailed by the Joachimites and Spirituals as a proof of God's detestation of the luxury of the Church. The treasure was returned, but by this time Boniface was implacable. All the weapons of the Holy War—the preaching of a crusade, excommunication, the inquisition—were turned against the Colonna. Their lands and castles were seized, their stronghold of Palestrina, full of precious relics of past ages, was razed to the ground. In the old Roman manner, the plough was passed over it, and salt sown on it. Ste-

phen Colonna, the new Scipio, wandered in exile, Jacopone da Todi was imprisoned. The two cardinals, in spite of a submission, which Boniface received in conclave, wearing the tiara "as a sign of the unity of the Church," were deprived. They passed, like Dante, from one refuge to another, and at last, like Stephen, made their way to France.

Boniface beat down these cardinals with the pitiless logic with which his predecessors had destroyed the Hohenstaufen, and a plausible defence of his action could doubtless be made; but a crusade against members of the Sacred College was so strange and monstrous that it raised in men's minds the issue of the moral responsibility of popes, not only to God, but to the Church. It was the heaviest count against a pope whom many regarded as a simoniac and were soon to regard as a heretic. Was it just that such a man should not be subject to the will of the Church? The possibility, admitted in theology, now threatened to become a very embarrassing fact. The moral issue is brought out clearly by Dante in his terrible verses on the tragedy of Palestrina. This prince of the new Pharisees was waging war not against Saracens or Jews, but in the neighbourhood of the Lateran. Every enemy of his was a Christian. Not one of them had helped to conquer Acre, the last Christian stronghold in Syria, not one of them had trafficked as a merchant in Egypt, a crime which at this time put a merchant outside the pale.

Dante drew a sharp distinction between the Pope and the man. . . . But Boniface too easily confused the Pope with Benedict Caetani. It is true that he kept apart the papal from his personal treasure, using the latter for the aggrandizement of his family. He was elected by cities of the Patrimony as their *podesta* under his family name. He arbitrated on one occasion between the kings of France and England—for so they insisted—not as pope but as Benedict. Yet this extraordinary man was incapable of self-scrutiny. As Mr. Previté-Orton has said, "the most ecumenic and the narrowest aims met one another in his violent nature, without apparently a suspicion arising in his mind of their discrepancy, and it was this attempt to blend incompatibles which more than anything else caused his ruin." . . . The type is not uncommon in history, but has only once been found upon the papal throne, varied though its occupants have been. Boniface had all the qualities of a very great pope save personal holiness and self-restraint. He was dignified and noble in appearance, decisive and vigorous, a master of business, a subtle canonist expert in explaining the meaning of terms and expounding the equitable rules of law. When he was not dominated by arrogance or passion, he could adjust himself to circumstance. "The coarse-mouthed bully" could "disappear for the moment in the skilful lawyer." His handling of the first controversy with Philip the Fair, opened in 1296 by the bull *Clericis laicos,* was reasonable, his compromise between facts and principles skilful. The distinguished lawyers who, under his commission, added the Sext or sixth book to the Decretals turned to him in cases of difficulty as an expert. His registers reveal in all its complexity the range of papal business to which he succeeded. . . . Boniface bore the responsibility of the insistent daily business suggested by the detailed life of this great establishment. A medieval pope might be as ascetic as St. Bernard, as unworldly as St. Francis, but he could not extricate himself, by a quick decision, from the duties of his supreme office, the accumulation of centuries, and insist that the most widespread and intricate of all governments, the framework and stay of all the activities of the Church, should be carried on by private inspiration, without revenues. To complain that Boniface was not a Celestine would be as absurd as to complain that Cromwell was not a Fifth Monarchy man. The real *gravamen* against Boniface was indeed the opposite of this, that, adequate though he was to the traditional task entrusted to him, he was the victim of his own temperament. He was like a man of the finest physical gifts but without that tiny cerebral instrument which enables him to keep his balance. . . . Petrarch described him as the wonder of kings and peoples, indeed of the world. He did everything either in the grand manner or with extravagant abandonment. He was so completely identified with the traditions of the papacy, that he felt at liberty to do as he liked. As a cardinal and legate he had rated the assembled doctors of Paris as though they were schoolboys. He once refused to confirm a metropolitan because he did not approve of his face, which may have been right; but he told him so, which was certainly wrong. He insulted ambassadors and mocked the physical peculiarities of his cardinals. This man, who celebrated Mass and said the offices with all the intensity of his being, even to tears, could fling the penitential ashes into the face of a Ghibelline archbishop. He had at his service the most learned and devoted apologists among the theologians and canonists of his age, but he had no friends. He was admired by many, feared by all, loved by none. He seems to have been untouched by the spiritual and intellectual influences in which most men find the meaning of their vocation in life. He took the vocation for granted. Cardinals, theologians, canonists were his instruments; he had quite enough to do with them in any case. In private he preferred the company of those who could amuse him, however worthless he might know them to be. By nature he was inclined to be sceptical and sardonic, and to laugh at the follies and credulity of those with whom he had to do. . . . He did not attack Spirituals and others because they were worse than other people, but because they opposed him and seemed likely to be a public danger. Then they became everything that was vile. Again, Boniface was not anti-French. His whole policy in Italy depended on French support. As a cardinal he had been suspected as a friend of France and he had his well-wishers in the French royal family; but when the French king and his advisers resisted his authority he was merciless. After the Jubilee of 1300, he put no restraint upon himself. The ambassador of Aragon wrote in 1301, "Everyone wishes he was dead and deplores the outrageous things he says and does." And the Englishman to whom we owe the best account of the attack on Anagni two years later tells how the whole country-side was roused against the Pope in his days of humiliation.

Rumour, inspired by hatred, quickly plays havoc with the reputation of such a man. The incredible *dossier* collected by his enemies after his death need not surprise us. The terms of the inquiry presented to the witnesses were drafted with great care, in the hope of avoiding all misunderstanding, but the witnesses were too carefully chosen and too sure of their ground to be embarrassed. Boniface had given them many openings, and the most harmless jibe could be used— probably quite conscientiously—as evidence of heresy. One day, for example, the admiral Roger Loria had rather

unctuously enlarged upon the joys awaiting him in Paradise. The pope caustically replied, "Maybe, maybe not." This was used to prove that Boniface did not believe in a future life. A recalcitrant French bishop was ordered to erect a statue of a pope, so that he might not again forget his duty to the Head of the Church. This was used to suggest that Boniface was an idolater. . . . We need not pay much heed to these charges, still less to the grosser accusations brought against Boniface. The truth is that he had a rough and caustic tongue, a brutal sense of humour, and an ungovernable temper, and that behind the lofty ecclesiasticism in which he so passionately believed, and of which he was such a dignified and vigorous exponent, there lurked the mundane passions, the curiosity, the love of fame, the self-confidence of a cultivated Italian nobleman. "He who is healthy, rich and fortunate," he is reported to have said, "has Paradise on earth." And one day he said to his physician, "We have increased the Roman Church in so much gold and silver, that our memory will be glorious for evermore."

Equal to every occasion, unhampered by self-questioning, Boniface moved on from his wars and vendettas, his dispute with France and his efforts to control the destiny of faction-ridden Florence, to the great year of the Jubilee. In this year 1300 he was, to all seeming, firm as a rock, as secure as any successor of St. Peter. Thousands of pilgrims passed daily from the shrine of St. Peter to the shrine of St. Paul. A plenary indulgence —hitherto granted only to crusaders— was open to all save the schismatics, Frederick of Sicily and the Colonna and the merchants who traded with the infidel. Christendom seemed to be united in Rome under the vicar of God. Boniface passed on to other triumphs. Towards the end of 1302 he put an end to the wasteful war with Sicily. Frederick was to hold the throne for life, but the island was afterwards to revert to the house of Anjou. The Pope could well afford the compromise, for he had his eyes on a greater vassal. In a consistory of 30 April 1303 he received the ambassadors of Albert of Austria, king of Germany and emperor elect. They brought royal letters confirming an oath of fealty, more far-reaching than any oath of any German king to a pope, before or since—an oath modelled on that given by the officers who governed the Papal States. . . . It was for the Pope to decide which favoured people should be the seat of empire. Albert's chancellor followed with a scholastic harangue in which he exalted the papal power and submitted to the papal doctrine. Then he and his colleagues took the oath on behalf of their master.

Within four months the servants of Philip of France and the fiercest of the Colonna had broken into the palace of Anagni. Within five months Boniface was dead. For ten years the Church was perplexed by the issue whether he was or was not a heretic and a criminal, subject, even in death, to the verdict of a council. Albert of Austria, quite unaffected, went on his astute way. He had got what he wanted, security of tenure. Rome resumed its life of family feuds and Italy its endless wars. And the popes, gradually realizing that their work could best be done elsewhere, settled down in Avignon.

When Boniface in the spring of 1303 came to an understanding with Albert of Austria he had for more than a year been involved in a hot dispute with Philip of France. The immediate cause was the proceedings of Philip against the bishop of Pamiers, a friend of the Pope:

this raised the issue of the immunity of the clergy, an issue which was soon developed to cover the whole question of the relations between the secular and ecclesiastical powers. The Pope was determined to fight to a finish—a wild ambition, for this issue has never been fought to a finish without the disintegration of Europe. His elaborate argumentation in the bull *Ausculta fili* (5 Dec. 1301) was treated with contempt —the rumour spread that it had been thrown on the fire. A misleading and abbreviated version—a medieval Ems telegram—was circulated. Its blunt phrasing—"It is our will that you be subject to us in temporal and spiritual things" —rallied the nobility of France, for St. Louis himself, whom Boniface had recently canonized, would have repudiated such doctrine. The clergy were disunited and hesitant. The States-General, meeting in Notre-Dame, supported the King. The Pope stood firm. He was encouraged by the disastrous defeat of the French army in Flanders in July 1302, he counted upon the support of Albert of Austria, Philip's former ally. Soon after a council held on All Saints' Day to which he had summoned the leading French clergy, he issued the bull *Unam Sanctam*. Philip temporized, whether from genuine hesitation or policy is still disputed. He offered to discuss the issues in dispute. The Pope, through his legate, demanded a definite answer and reminded him that, by putting obstacles in the way of free intercourse between Rome and France, he was already excommunicate. The King, in June 1303, appealed to a council of the Church. Throughout France his emissaries secured the adhesion of local governments and towns. He could rely on the nobles and most of the secular clergy, and even the Franciscans were equally divided between king and pope.

The national rally against Pope Boniface was largely due to a man who, after some years in the royal service, had lately won the ear of the King. This was William of Nogaret, a native of the country of Toulouse, and a former professor of law in Montpellier. There is no good ground to reject the story that William's father and mother had been burned as heretics. He came from a land full of bitter memories. He belonged to a people whose sceptical, but passionate, outlook had no room for the tenacious orthodoxy and disciplined traditions which made compromise in its relations with the Church almost a matter of principle at the French court. Nogaret was a clerk in minor orders, *magister* as well as *miles regis;* he could quote Scripture and St. Augustine with the facility of a schoolman; he professed at every turn to be serving the true interests of the Church; and he had a very definite idea of the part which the king of France, the eldest son of the Church, should play. He was more obstinate than Boniface himself, and he was carried along by a cold fury more sinister and dreadful than Boniface's hot passion. . . .

Dramatic symbolism, which coloured the mind of men in those days, gave the life of Boniface a setting of thunder and darkness. When in 1291 he said his first Mass at Orvieto, and more candles were lit in the church because of the darkness of the day, men saw an augury of schism and war. A thunderstorm appropriately cut short the ceremony of his burial. Stories of his last days, of his madness and despair and blasphemies, were spread abroad. For ten years a dismal warfare was waged against his memory, while he lay in the splendid tomb which Arnolfo di Cambio at his command had prepared for him in the church of St. Peter. But now, in Renan's fine phrase, he has entered into the serenity of history; and we can see him more clearly, a man who, if he had not been the victim of his own impulses, might have been planned by nature to be the master of the world.

Boniface, unhappily for himself, lived in a time which needed a pope as great as himself but wiser, more temperate, more far-seeing. It was a time when the rich experience of the past was in flower, when poets and artists, mystics, theologians and canonists, princes and statesmen, travellers and merchants, were becoming conscious of their inheritance, when the creative and reflective powers were free and new horizons were opening. We should not set one activity against another as more far-reaching or more enlightened, for all alike were rooted in the past, and opened out under the same sky. . . . At no time in history have more fine spirits been alive to the riches of the visible and the invisible. And at no time were men more aware of the dangers which beset the unity of the Christian world, as the wealth of experience, the rights of states, the infinite possibilities of commerce and money and social life were revealed. In the long discipline of centuries all this richness had been stored, and now the unity which it had been the object of the Church to conserve and enrich was threatened by the Church's own children. Boniface was not the man to guide Europe into the way of peace, or to unite Christendom in a Holy War, but, in his efforts to do so, he was sustained by forces far greater and purer than his own imperious will. He had behind him the traditions of the medieval Church.

Suggestions for Further Reading

There is an enormous literature on the quarrels of Boniface VIII and Philip the Fair, which in its variety is illustrative of the reasons why people write history. One of the first books to appear on the subject, for example, was Pierre Dupuy, *Histoire du différend d'entre le pape Boniface VIII et Philippes le Bel, roy de France* (Paris, 1655; reprinted Phoenix, Ariz., 1963), a fundamental work, since Dupuy prints nearly all the documents and chronicles of importance to the dispute. Dupuy was the court bibliographer of Louis XIV, and his work reflects that monarch's insistence on the continued liberties of the Gallican Church. As a result, Boniface comes off rather badly in the short narrative account that introduces the documents.

It was not until the nineteenth century that anyone was found to support the papal position, but when this happened Boniface's sympathizers turned out to be as vociferous as Philip's. Typical here is Dom Luigi Tosti, *Storia di Bonifacio VIII* (Monte Cassino, 1846), translated as *History of Pope Boniface and His Times* (New York, 1911), a work that is more notable for its apologetics than for its scholarship. Much more credible, though still favorable to the pope, is the more recent work of Sister Mary Mildred Curley, *The Conflict between Boniface VIII and Philip IV, the Fair* (Washington, D.C., 1927).

It was also in the nineteenth century that modern historical scholarship began, in the sense that those engaged in research began consciously to try to present an objective analysis, not merely a polemic argued from those pieces of evidence that happened to sustain their points of view. During the latter half of the century many articles appeared on specific aspects of the quarrel and no longer

had as their primary aim the justification of one or the other of the chief protagonists. These articles are discussed below. It should be noted that they were first synthesized in Heinrich Finke, *Aus den Tagen Bonifaz VIII: Funde and Forschungen* (Münster, 1902; reprinted 1964), a series of essays that is really the start of modern work on the subject. More recent books, such as T. S. R. Boase, *Boniface VIII* (London, 1933) and August Baumhauer, *Philipp der Schöne und Bonifaz VIII in ihrer Stellung zur französischen Kirche* (Freiburg-im-Breisgau, 1920), owe much to this pioneering volume. At the same time, of course, it became possible to get further into the issues simply because more of the necessary documents were being published and made available. Notable in this endeavor was Georges Digard, one of those most actively engaged in publication of the official registers of Boniface VIII; his *Philippe le Bel et le Saint-Siège de 1285 à 1304* (2 vols.; Paris, 1936) is the logical culmination of more than a generation's detailed research and is the latest and most complete examination of the total problem.

At the same time, as F. M. Powicke remarks in *The Christian Life in the Middle Ages* (Oxford, England, 1933), from which a selection appears in this book, much work was being done in the whole field of medieval history and political theory, and it has helped to modify our understanding of the particular issues involved in the battles between Boniface and Philip. Actually, the reader would probably be well advised to begin any further study of the problem with an investigation of some of the better treatments of medieval political theory and practice, all of which at least allude to the specifics involved in the pontificate of Boniface VIII. The classic work in this regard is A. J. and R. W. Carlyle, *A History of Mediaeval Political Theory in the West* (6 vols.; London, 1903–1936), volume V of which is of special relevance to the thirteenth and early fourteenth centuries. Possibly more useful for the beginning student is the more recent *History of Political Theory* by George Sabine (3d ed.; New York, 1961) which traces political thought from the Greeks to the twentieth century. A recent work which takes a more institutional and less theoretical approach is Norman Zacour, *An Introduction to Medieval Institutions* (New York, 1969). For both the theory and practice of papal government, see John A. Watt, *The Theory of Papal Monarchy in the Thirteenth Century: The Contribution of the Canonists* (New York, 1966); further, the various studies of Walter Ullmann all deserve mention: *Medieval Papalism: The Political Theories of the Medieval Canonists* (London, 1949); *The Growth of Papal Government in the Middle Ages* (London, 1955); and *Principles of Government and Politics in the Middle Ages* (London, 1961), a broader and more general book that attempts to look at the theoretical justifications offered by both the secular and spiritual powers. Also of value is Brian Tierney, *The Crisis of Church and State, 1050–1300* (Englewood Cliffs, N.J., 1964), a collection of documents with extended commentary. In particular, Tierney translates and publishes most of the key bulls of Boniface VIII as well as various related pieces, such as one of the proclamations of the Colonna cardinals against the pope.

By far the largest part of the literature is devoted to specific aspects of the relations between king and pope. Naturally enough, much effort has been devoted to the careers and views of the people actually involved. Here, however, there are surprising gaps. Philip the Fair has still to receive a full-dress twentieth-century treatment, although the question of his personal responsibility for the actions of his government is a problem that has long fascinated scholars. Among the more interesting interpretations are: Heinrich Finke, "Zur Charakteristik Philipps des Schönen," *Mitteilungen des Instituts für* *österreichische Geschichtsforschung*, XXVI (1905), 201–224; and K. Wenck, *Philipp der Schöne von Frankreich* (Marburg, 1905). The most recent work—and the most fully documented case for Philip's personal involvement—is J. R. Strayer, "Philip the Fair—A 'Constitutional' King," *American Historical Review*, LXII (1956), 18–32, reprinted in the present work, but interested readers should also consult Robert Fawtier, *L'Europe occidentale de 1270 à 1380*, volume VI[1] of G. Glotz, *Histoire générale* (Paris, 1940), especially pp. 298–302.

Lesser figures, too, have come in for their share of attention. Information is sketchy for most of Philip's ministers and agents, but a few studies exist, notably Robert Holtzmann, *Wilhelm von Nogaret* (Freiburg-im-Breisgau, 1898). Also of interest are: Abel Henry, "Guillaume de Plaisians, ministre de Philippe le Bel," *Le Moyen Âge*, V (1892), 32–38; Franklin Pegues, *The Lawyers of the Last Capetians* (Princeton, N.J., 1962); Jan Rogozinski, "Counsellors of the Seneschal of Beaucaire and Nimes, 1250–1350," *Speculum*, XLIV (1969), 421–439; and Joseph R. Strayer's forthcoming monograph, *Les gens de justice du Languedoc sous Philippe le Bel*. Much more has been published, however, on the French propagandists, whether officially sponsored or not. One of the better works on the subject is Ernest Renan, *Études sur la politique religieuse du règne de Philippe le Bel* (Paris, 1899); this is actually nothing more than a reprint of his articles on Nogaret, Dubois, and Bertrand de Got (the future Clement V) in *Histoire littéraire de la France*, volumes XXVI–XXVIII. Of much more fundamental importance is Richard Scholz, *Die Publizistik zur Zeit Philipps des Schönen und Bonifaz VIII* (Stuttgart, 1903). The best—and most exhaustive—study of Dubois is Ernst Zeck, *Der Publizist Pierre Dubois* (Berlin, 1911), but all except the most determined scholars will be well content with F. M. Powicke, "Pierre Dubois, a Medieval Radical," in T. F. Tout and James Tait, *Historical Essays* (Manchester, 1907). Charles-Victor Langlois has edited an important text on the publicists: "Satire cléricale du temps de Philippe le Bel," *Le Moyen Âge*, V (1892),

146ff, but the best general monographic treatment of the subject remains Helene Wieruszowski, *Vom Imperium zum nationalem Königtum, vergleichende Studien über die publizistischen Kämpfe Kaiser Friedrichs II und König Philipps des schönen mit der Kurie* (Munich and Berlin, 1933; reprinted Munich, 1965). Charles-Victor Langlois has inventoried and edited most of Nogaret's and Plaisians' surviving documents in two articles, "Les papiers de Guillaume de Nogaret et de Guillaume de Plaisians au Trésor de Chartes," *Notices et extraits des manuscrits de la Bibliothèque Nationale et autres bibliothèques,* XXXIX[1] (1909), 211–254; and "Autographes nouveaux de Guillaume de Nogaret," *Journal des Savants* (1917), 321–327.

Less has been done with the Italians involved in the controversy, although Boniface himself naturally receives a great deal of study in nearly every work. There is one detailed monograph on the Colonna cardinals and their role in the affairs of the Church: Ludwig Mohler, *Die Kardinäle Jacob und Peter Colonna: ein Beitrag zur Geschichte des Zeitalter Bonifaz' VIII.* (Paderborn, 1914), volume XVII of *Quellen und Forschungen aus dem Gebeite der Geschichte.* A broader study of the Curia during this period is to be found in Heinz Göring, *Die Beamten der Kurie unter Bonifaz VIII* (Königsberg, 1934). On the papal theorists, the works of Ullmann, already cited, are useful, as are the discussions, particularly of Egidius Romanus (Giles of Rome), in Charles H. McIlwain, *The Growth of Political Thought in the West* (New York, 1932). Also quite useful is M. J. Wilks, *The Problem of Sovereignty in the Later Middle Ages* (Cambridge, England, 1963), a book whose title is somewhat misleading since it is primarily a study of the papalist Augustinus Triumphus. It does, however, treat of the other theorists and publicists and contains an excellent bibliography for further research.

Each of the specific steps on the road to Anagni has received detailed attention, and a rough measure of each incident's importance and of the extent to which scholars agree or disagree on what happened may be gained simply by looking at the relative length of the literature on each subject. Since it was a unique event and led to so many of Boniface's later difficulties, Celestine V's renunciation of the papacy has been examined many times. In terms of the later disputes with France, probably the most interesting piece is the article by Dom Jean Leclercq used in the present book. As Leclercq points out, theological opinion firmly supported Celestine's right to resign and the legitimacy of Boniface's accession, but it did so in such a way that it continued to allow the possibility of a council's deposition of a pope for heresy. This point of view opened the way for Philip, as we have seen, but it may also have laid the groundwork for later conciliar theories at the time of the Great Schism. This possibility is explored by H. X. Arquillière, "L'appel au concile sous Philippe le Bel et la genèse des théories conciliaires," *Revue des questions historiques,* LXXXIX (1911), 23–55.

Since much of the most outspoken criticism of Boniface VIII arose from the ranks of the Spiritual Franciscans, the reader may wish to learn more about them. The whole nature of the movement and of the apocalyptic extremes to which its writings could go are well illustrated in D. L. Douie, *The Nature and the Effect of the Heresy of the Fratricelli* (Manchester, 1932); though somewhat flawed and outdated, this remains a good general survey of the subject. A more recent study of the origins of this movement is to be found in E. Randolph Daniel, "A Re-Examination of the Origins of Franciscan Joachitism," *Speculum,* XLIII (1968), 671–676.

On Boniface's Jubilee there is less literature, a characteristic study being H. Thurston, S.J., *The Holy Year of Jubilee* (New York, 1900), an attempt to see papal jubilees within the context of broader religious thought and purpose. With *Ausculta fili* there is a revival of interest and controversy, particularly on the reception this bull was accorded in France. Here the key articles are Félix Rocquain, "Philippe le Bel et la bulle *Ausculta fili,*" *Bibliothèque de l'École des Chartes,* XLIV (1883), 393–418; and Robert Holtzmann, "Philipp der Schöne von Frankreich und die

Bulle *Ausculta fili,*" *Deutsche Zeitschrift für Geschichtswissenschaft* [now called the *Historische Vierteljahrschrift*], Neue Folge, II (1897), 16–38. Among other things, Holtzmann argues that the French had *Ausculta fili* publicly burned, whereas Rocquain maintains that there is not enough evidence to prove this point. A totally different argument is advanced by Barthélémy Pocquet du Haut-Jussé in his "Seconde différence entre Boniface VIII et Philippe le Bel," *Melanges . . . Albert Dufourcq* (Paris, 1932), 73–108; if Pocquet du Haut-Jussé is to be believed, Philip was a man aggrieved because Boniface had succeeded in monopolizing the appointment of all bishops in France.

Needless to say, *Unam Sanctam* has attracted frequent detailed examination. There is an excellent bibiography in Jean Rivière, *Le problème de l'église et de l'état au temps de Philippe le Bel* (Paris and Louvain, 1926), whose own analysis has been used in the present book. The range of opinion is enormous, going from the view that the bull is a forgery (P. Mury, "La bulle *Unam Sanctam,*" *Revue des questions historiques,* XXVI [1879], 41–130; XLVI [1889], 253–257, the latter article being a retraction that followed the publication of Boniface's relevant register) to the highly abstract treatment of the Germans (J. Berchtold, *Die Bulle Unam Sanctam* [Munich, 1887]). The work of Digard, already cited, probably gives the most balanced analysis, though in a recent paper Richard Kay has added a new dimension to the issues involved. Arguing that the meeting of bishops preceding the issuance of *Unam Sanctam* is better to be regarded as a convocation than a formal council of the Church, Kay then implies that Boniface intended not to condemn Philip, but only to reply in a suitable manner to the equally informal assemblies that the king had held earlier in 1302. This paper, "*Ad nostram praesentiam evocamus:* Boniface VIII and the Convocation of French Prelates to Rome, November 1302," is scheduled soon to be published in the *Proceedings of the Institute of Medieval Canon Law.*

At present Anagni appears to be the fiercest • of the scholarly battlegrounds. The Italian view tends to blame the French in a veiled way, as witness P. Fedele, "Per la storia dell' attentato de Anagnia," *Bulletino dell' Istituto storico italiano per il medio evo* (1921), 195ff. Robert Fawtier has counterattacked in his "L'attentat d'Anagni," *Mélanges d'archéologie et d'histoire,* LX (1948), 153–179, reprinted in the present volume. The standard article on the subject is W. Holtzmann, "Zum Attentat von Anagni," *Festschrift . . . Albert Brackmann* (Weimar, 1931), 492–507; but Holtzmann's conclusions must be modified in light of Henry G. J. Beck's critical edition and translation, "William Hundleby's Account of the Anagni Outrage," *Catholic Historical Review,* XXXII (1947), 190–220. Fawtier's ·interpretation has naturally been hotly opposed, notably by Marion Melville, "Guillaume de Nogaret et Philippe le Bel," *Revue d'histoire et de l'église de France,* XXXVI (1950), 56–66. There the matter rests for the moment, although there is certain to be further study.

Lastly, something should be said about the events that followed Boniface's death. Philip's continued attacks on his late adversary's memory as well as on the Order of the Knights Templar are well treated in Georges Lizerand, *Clément V et Philippe le Bel* (Paris, 1910), a monograph that has an extensive, though now dated, bibliography. On the "Babylonian Captivity," certainly another very concrete result of Philip's defeat of the papacy, the standard work is Guillaume Mollat, *The Popes at Avignon, 1305–1378* (9th ed. London, 1963), also available in paperback from Harper Torchbooks (New York, 1965). Mollat, unlike earlier scholars of the period, has recognized the extent to which the Avignonese popes were not merely the creatures of the kings of France and has emphasized the variety of difficulties which kept them from returning to Rome. This being the case, one may continue to wonder, then, whether Philip the Fair's defeat of Boniface VIII was as complete and decisive as the average popular account would lead one to believe. And so the debate on significance continues.